THE GREAT BIG FUN WORKBOOK FOR MINECRAFTERS

Grades 3 & 4

Illustrated by Amanda Brack

Sky Pony Press
New York

Sky Pony Press books may be purchased in bulk at special discounts for sales promotion, corporate gifts, fund-raising, or educational purposes. Special editions can also be created to specifications. For details, contact the Special Sales Department, Sky Pony Press, 307 West 36th Street, 11th Floor, New York, NY 10018 or info@skyhorsepublishing.com.

Sky Pony® is a registered trademark of Skyhorse Publishing, Inc.®, a Delaware corporation.

Minecraft® is a registered trademark of Notch Development AB.
The Minecraft game is copyright © Mojang AB.

Visit our website at www.skyponypress.com.

Authors, books, and more at SkyPonyPressBlog.com.

10 9 8 7 6 5 4 3 2 1

Cover design by Brian Peterson

Interior art by Amanda Brack

Puzzles created by Jen Funk Weber

Book design by Kevin Baier

Print ISBN: 978-1-5107-3985-7

Printed in China

A NOTE TO PARENTS

Welcome to a great big world of fun and learning with a Minecrafting twist. When you want to reinforce classroom skills, break up screen time, or enhance kids' problem-solving skills at home, it's crucial to have high-interest, kid-friendly learning materials. *The Great Big Fun Workbook for Minecrafters* transforms educational lessons into exciting adventures complete with diamond swords, zombies, skeletons, and creepers. With colorful illustrations and familiar characters to guide them through, your kids will feel like winners from start to finish.

This mega-fun workbook is organized into six distinct chapters targeting a wide variety of math, problem-solving, and language arts skills. Inside you'll find exercises in math basics like skip counting; mazes, games, and puzzles to help develop their problem-solving skills; guided cursive instruction; and reading comprehension activities. Use the table of contents to pinpoint areas for extra practice!

Now for the best part: The educational content in this workbook is aligned with National Common Core Standards for 3rd and 4th grade. What does that mean, exactly? Everything in this book matches up with what children are learning or will be learning in 3rd and 4th grade. This eliminates confusion, builds confidence, and keeps them ahead of the curve.

Whether it's the joy of seeing their favorite game come to life on each page or the thrill of solving challenging problems just like Steve and Alex, there is something in *The Great Big Fun Workbook for Minecrafters* to entice every student.

Happy adventuring!

 # CONTENTS

Math for Minecrafters

Games and Puzzles for Minecrafters

Language Arts for Minecrafters

MATH FOR MINECRAFTERS

MULTIPLICATION, DIVISION, AND MORE!

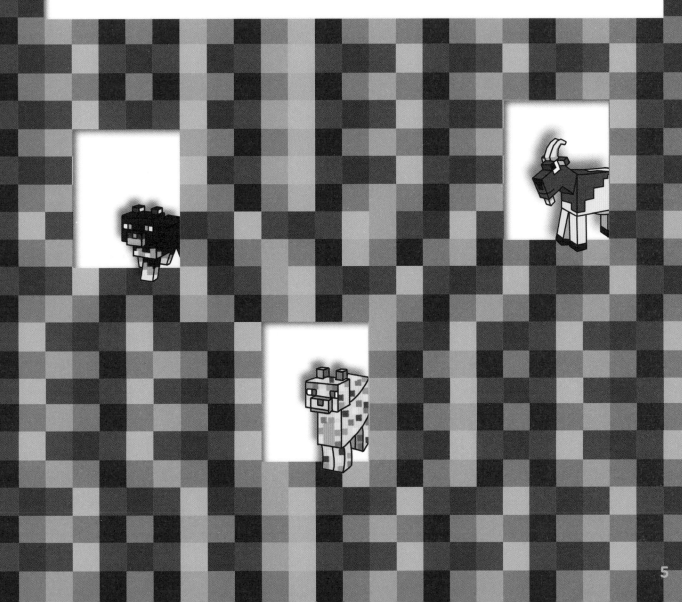

MULTIPLICATION BY GROUPING

Write the multiplication sentence that matches the picture.
Then solve the equation.

Example: **Answer:**

1. $\underline{2} \times \underline{10} = \underline{20}$

2. _____ × _____ = _____

3. _____ × _____ = _____

4. _____ × _____ = _____

5. _____ × _____ = _____

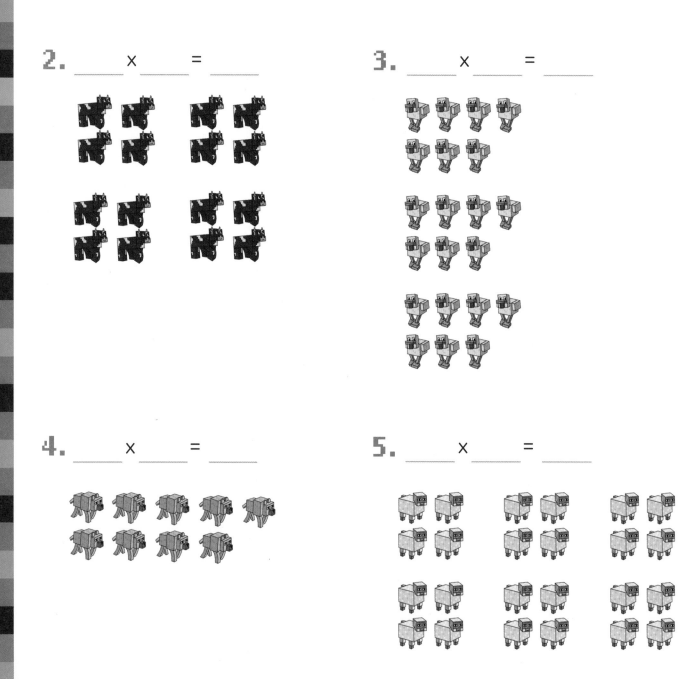

MYSTERY MESSAGE
WITH MULTIPLICATION

Multiply. Then use the letters to fill in the blanks below and reveal the answer to the joke.

1. 4 x 8 = 32   A

2. 2 x 6 = ___   D

3. 6 x 3 = ___   Y

4. 3 x 8 = ___   C

5. 7 x 5 = ___   S

6. 8 x 5 = ___   O

7. 8 x 2 = ___   E

8. 9 x 6 = ___   R

9. 10 x 3 = ___   T

Q: Where does a baby creeper go when his parents are at work?
COPY THE LETTERS FROM THE ANSWERS ABOVE TO FIND OUT.

He goes

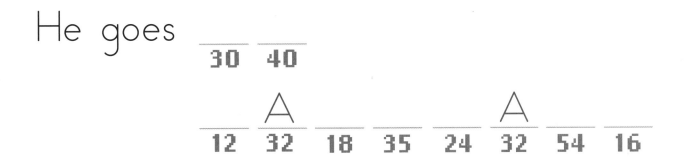

30 40

___ A ___ ___ ___ A ___ ___
12 32 18 35 24 32 54 16

ZOMBIE'S GUIDE TO PLACE VALUE

Write the number on each zombie in expanded form in the space provided.

Example:  **Answer:**

1.
1,360

$1,000 + 300 + 60 + 0$

2.
4,672

_____

3.
2,798

_____

4.
8,540

_____

5.
3,151

_____

6.
6,736

_____

7.
5,459

_____

MATH FACTS CHALLENGE

Find the pattern and fill in the empty spaces to help Alex escape the zombie.

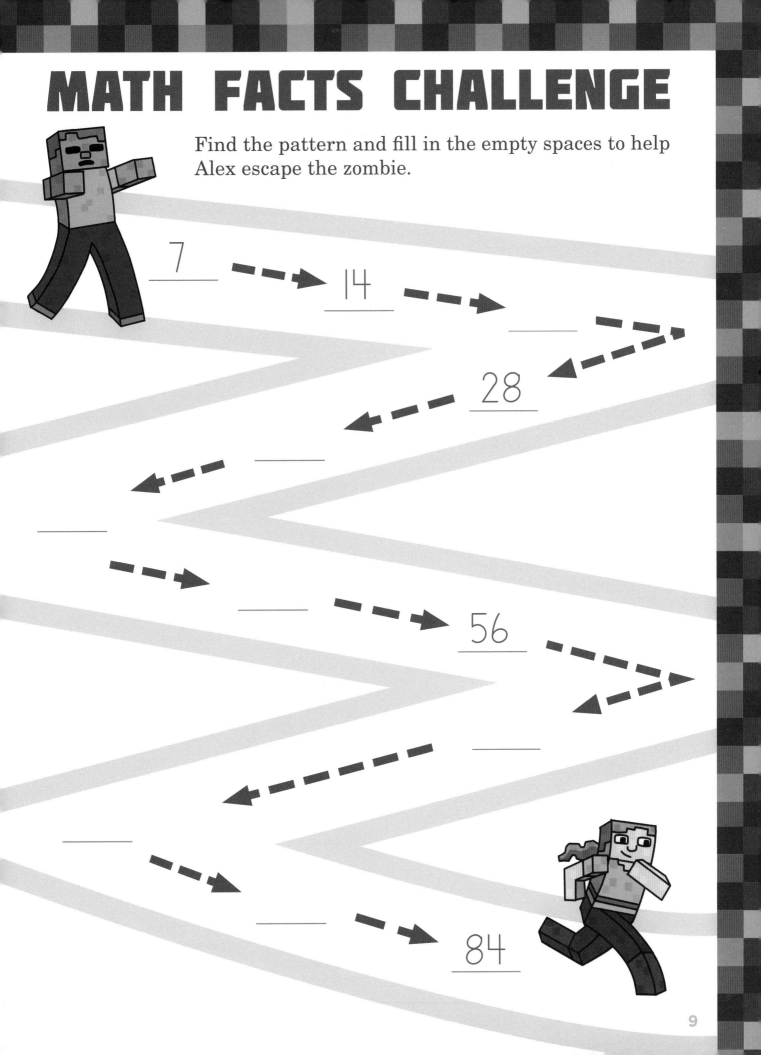

7 → 14 → ___ → 28 → ___ → ___ → ___ → 56 → ___ → ___ → ___ → 84

TELLING TIME

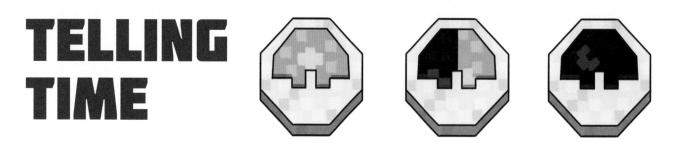

Look at the clocks below and write the time in the space provided:

Example:

1.

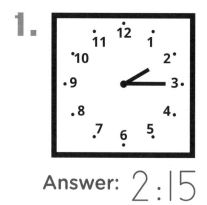

Answer: 2:15

2.

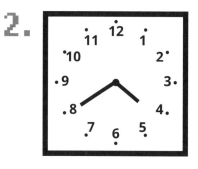

Answer: _____

3.

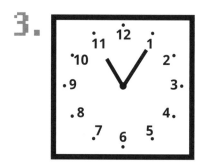

Answer: _____

4.

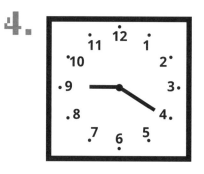

Answer: _____

5.

Answer: _____

6.

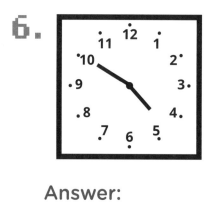

Answer: _____

THE TRADING TABLE

The villagers have emeralds to give Alex in exchange for her food items. Look at the table below to solve the problems that follow.

FARMER	🟩	🟩	🟩	🟩			
LIBRARIAN	🟩	🟩					
BLACKSMITH	🟩	🟩	🟩				
BUTCHER	🟩	🟩	🟩	🟩	🟩	🟩	

Write the amount of emeralds next to each villager using the table above.

1 pile of emeralds = 8 emeralds.

1. The **farmer** villager has _____ .

2. The **librarian** villager has _____ .

3. The **blacksmith** villager has _____ .

4. The **butcher** villager has _____ .

5. Which villagers have more emeralds than the **blacksmith** villager? _____

6. Which villager has the least amount of emeralds? _____

7. The **librarian** wants to have as many emeralds as the **butcher**. Which villager's collection does he need to add to his? _____

GEOMETRY SKILLS PRACTICE

How many items are in each array? Count the number of items in one row and one column. Write a multiplication sentence to find the answer.

Example:

1. $\underline{2}$ x $\underline{5}$ = $\underline{10}$

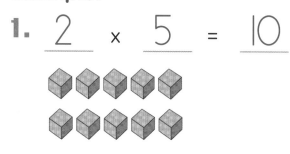

2. _____ x _____ = _____

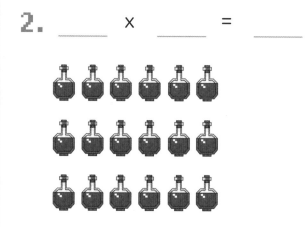

3. _____ x _____ = _____

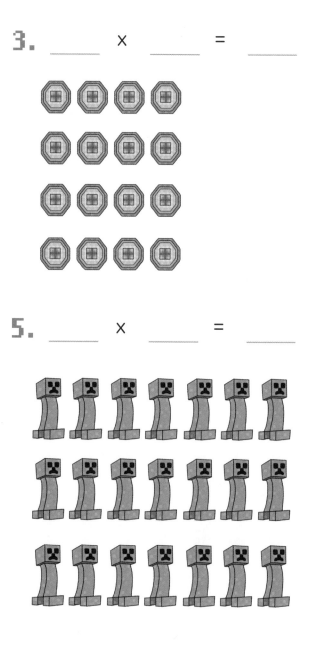

4. _____ x _____ = _____

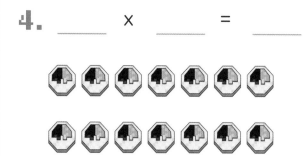

5. _____ x _____ = _____

6. _____ x _____ = _____

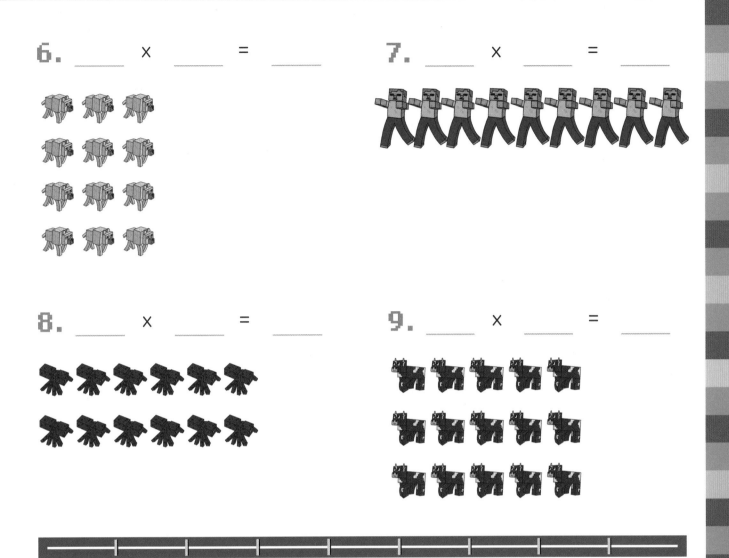

7. _____ x _____ = _____

8. _____ x _____ = _____

9. _____ x _____ = _____

HARDCORE MODE: Try this hardcore math challenge!

_____ x _____ = _____ + _____ = _____

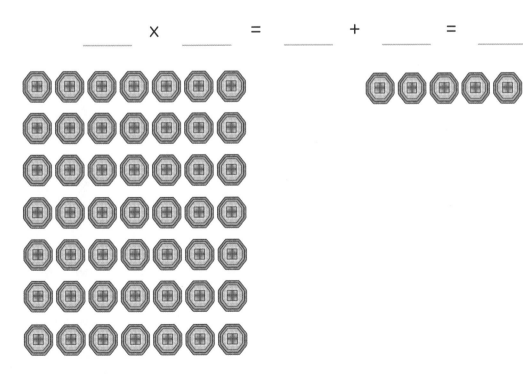

MULTIPLICATION WORD PROBLEMS

Read the problem carefully. Draw a picture or write a number sentence to help you solve the problem.

Example:

1. A creeper blows up 2 cows every time it explodes. How many cows will be killed by 3 exploding creepers?

Answer: 6 cows

$$3 \times 2 = 6$$

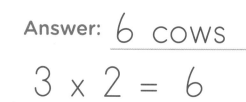

2. In order to make 1 cake, you need 3 buckets of milk. How many buckets of milk do you need to make 2 cakes?

Answer: _____

3. One block of wood is enough to make 4 planks of wood. If you have 4 blocks of wood, how many planks can you make?

Answer: _____

4. One ocelot drops 3 experience orbs for you to collect. How many experience orbs can you collect from 6 ocelots?

Answer: _____

5. You need 6 sandstone blocks to craft 1 set of stairs. How many sandstone blocks do you need to build 7 sets of stairs?

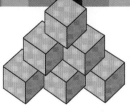

Answer: _____

6. One cow drops 3 pieces of raw beef. How many pieces of raw beef can you get from 4 cows?

Answer: _____

7. One full day in the game world is the same as 20 minutes in the real world. If you spend 5 days in Alex's world, how many real-world minutes go by?

Answer: _____

8. Steve needs 9 fish to tame an ocelot. How many fish does he need to tame 3 ocelots?

Answer: _____

9. It takes 4 bottles of potion to survive a hostile mob attack. How many bottles of potion do you need to survive 6 mob attacks?

Answer: _____

GHAST'S GUIDE TO PLACE VALUE

Answer the multiplication questions below.
Then round to the closest ten.

Solve It!   **Round It!**

1. 2 x 3 =   6   10

2. 4 x 9 = _____   _____

3. 6 x 8 = _____   _____

4. 3 x 5 = _____   _____

5. 7 x 4 = _____   _____

6. 8 x 5 = _____   _____

7. 9 x 7 = _____   _____

MATH FACTS CHALLENGE

Count by 4 and practice your math facts to help Steve escape the wither!

4 → 8 → ___ → ___ → ___ → ___ → ___ → ___ → ___ → ___ → 48

MINUTE HAND MYSTERY

A computer glitch erased the minute hands from these clocks! Solve the problem to find out how many minutes have passed, then draw in the minute hand.

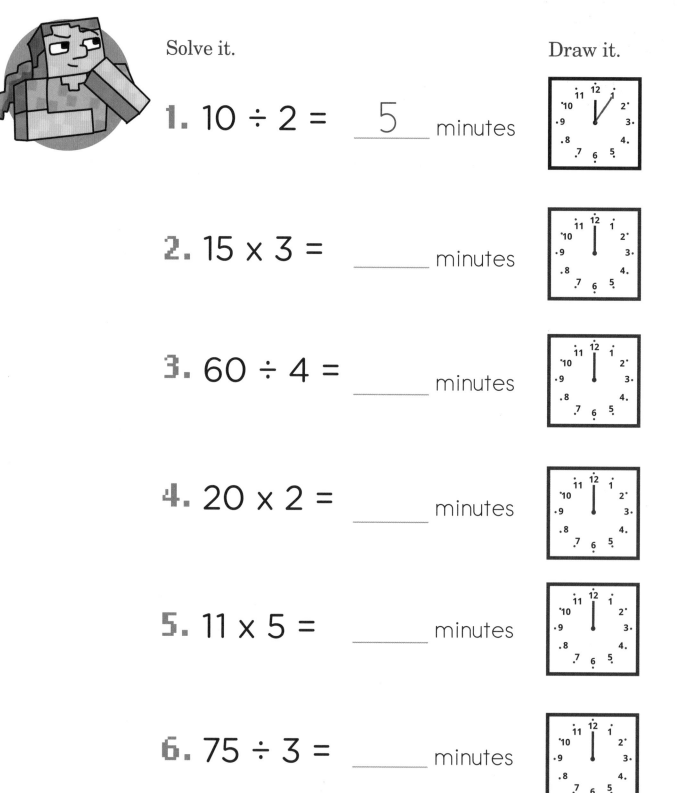

Solve it.

Draw it.

1. 10 ÷ 2 = _____5_____ minutes

2. 15 x 3 = _____ minutes

3. 60 ÷ 4 = _____ minutes

4. 20 x 2 = _____ minutes

5. 11 x 5 = _____ minutes

6. 75 ÷ 3 = _____ minutes

EQUAL TRADE

This librarian villager loves trading for new coins. Figure out the right number of coins to trade so that you don't lose any money in the deal.

1. How many **pennies** equal 1 dime?  Answer: _____

2. How many **nickels** equal 1 quarter? Answer: _____

3. How many **pennies** equal 3 nickels?  Answer: _____

4. How many **quarters** equal a dollar? Answer: _____

5. How many **dimes** equal 2 quarters? Answer: _____

ADVENTURES IN GEOMETRY

Which of these gaming images are symmetrical? Circle them.

Symmetrical = an object that can be divided with a line into two matching halves.

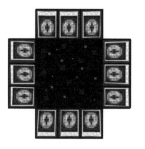

CREATIVE MODE

Complete the other half of this drawing to make it as symmetrical as possible:

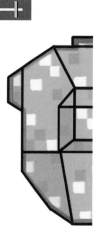

SHELTER GEOMETRY

Alex and Steve have been working all afternoon to build a new shelter out of redstone blocks.

Area=
height x width

1. Calculate the area of Alex's wall:

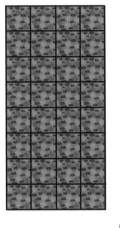

_____ x _____ = _____

2. Calculate the area of Steve's wall:

_____ x _____ = _____

3. Which player's wall has the greatest area? _____

4. How many more blocks did that player use? _____

5. If you combine their two walls, what would the area of their new, larger wall be? _____

MULTIPLICATION BY GROUPING

Count each group of 3, then finish the equation to find the answer.

1. 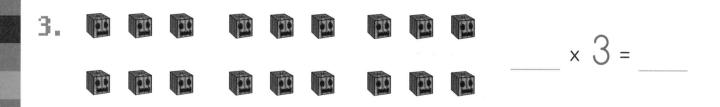 _____ x 3 = _____

2. 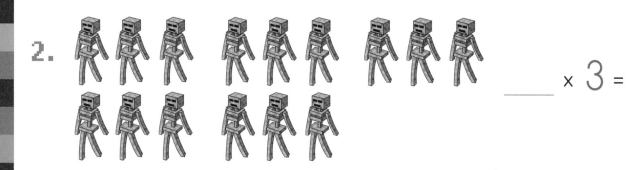 _____ x 3 = _____

3. _____ x 3 = _____

4. _____ x 3 = _____

5. 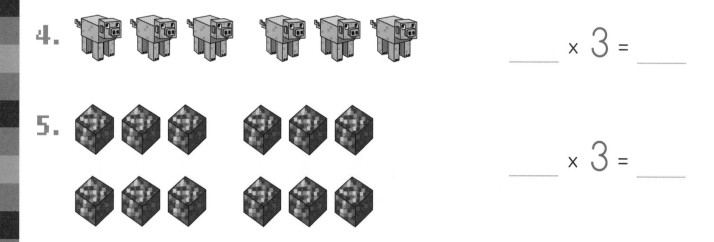 _____ x 3 = _____

MYSTERY MESSAGE
WITH MULTIPLICATION AND DIVISION

Solve the problems below to find out which number matches with which letter. Then put the correct letters into the message to answer the riddle!

1. $234 \div 2 =$ ___117___ E

2. $34 \times 3 =$ ___ ___ O

3. $77 \times 4 =$ ___ ___ H

4. $434 \div 7 =$ ___ ___ R

5. $165 \times 5 =$ ___ ___ B

6. $924 \div 4 =$ ___ ___ N

7. $201 \times 3 =$ ___ ___ I

Q: What mysterious character looks like Steve but has glowing white eyes?

COPY THE LETTERS FROM THE ANSWERS ABOVE TO FIND OUT.

___308___ ___117___ ___62___ ___102___ ___825___ ___62___ ___603___ ___231___ ___117___

ENDERMAN'S GUIDE TO PLACE VALUE

Solve the multiplication equations below. Match each answer to the correct place value description on the right.

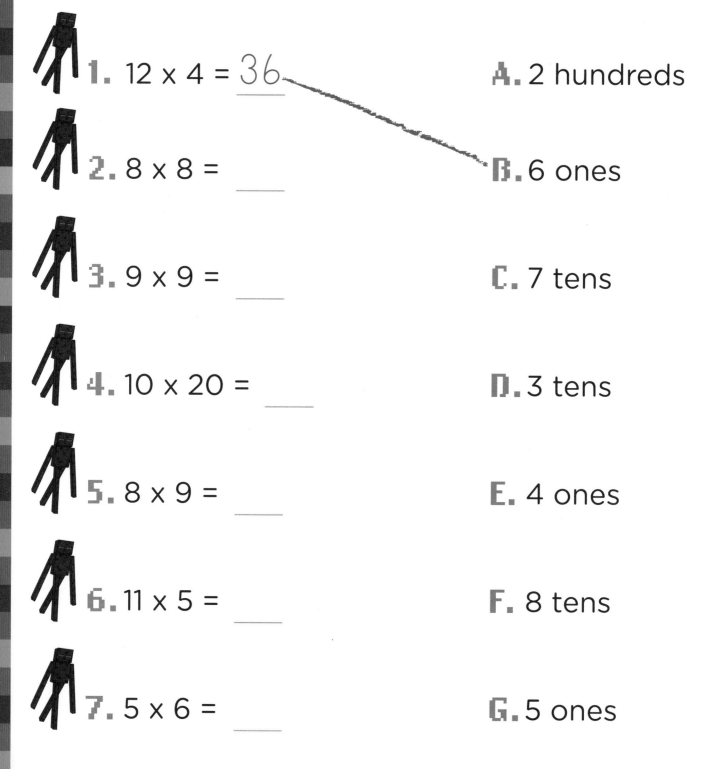

1. 12 x 4 = 36 _____

2. 8 x 8 = _____

3. 9 x 9 = _____

4. 10 x 20 = _____

5. 8 x 9 = _____

6. 11 x 5 = _____

7. 5 x 6 = _____

A. 2 hundreds

B. 6 ones

C. 7 tens

D. 3 tens

E. 4 ones

F. 8 tens

G. 5 ones

SKIP COUNT CHALLENGE

Thanks to the lure enchantment, you catch 9 pufferfish every time you go fishing! Pretty soon, you'll have enough to tame your ocelot. Count by 9 to find out how many pufferfish you'll catch at the end of the day.

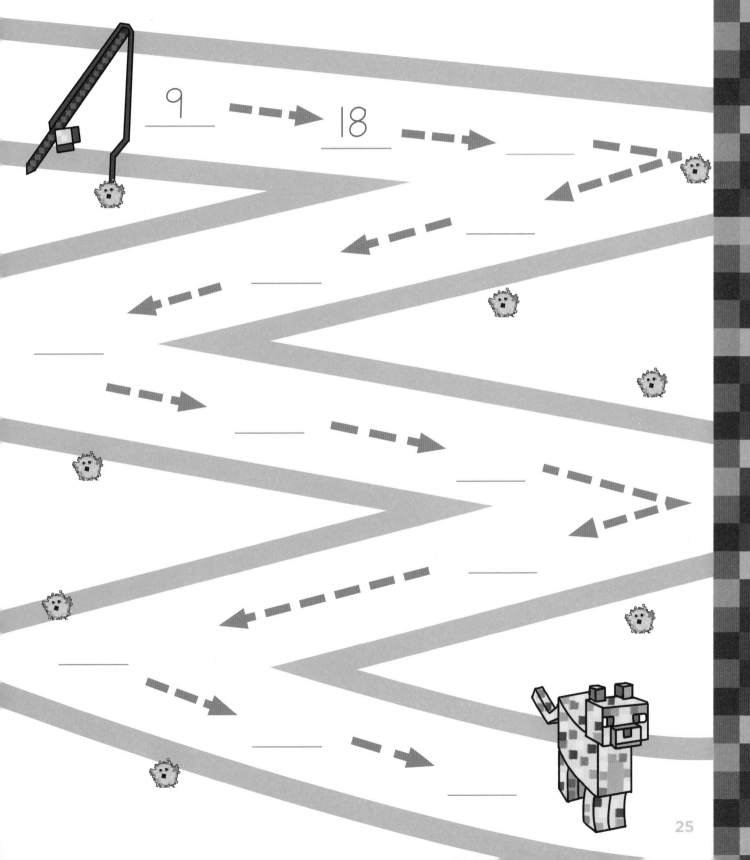

TELLING TIME

The mooshroom is teaching his baby how to tell time, but he needs your help. Help the baby mooshroom by writing down the correct time next to each clock.

Example:

1.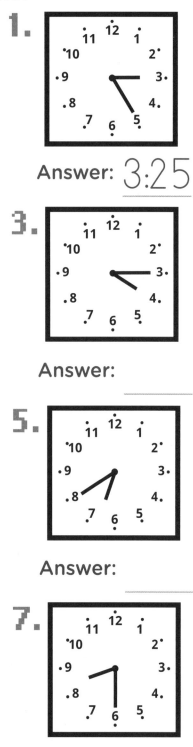

Answer: 3:25

2.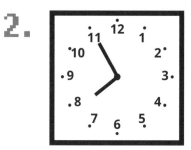

Answer: _____

3.

Answer: _____

4.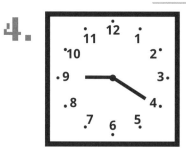

Answer: _____

5.

Answer: _____

6.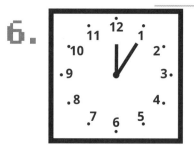

Answer: _____

7.

Answer: _____

8.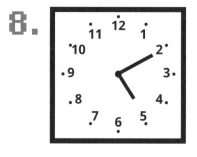

Answer: _____

26

SPAWN EGG CHALLENGE

Solve the equations next to each colored bucket to find out how many exploding creepers will soon be hatching from the buckets. Then run!

1. $27 \times 5 =$ _____

2. $120 \div 6 =$ _____

3. $94 \times 2 =$ _____

4. $39 \times 2 =$ _____

5. $320 \div 8 =$ _____

6. $53 \times 4 =$ _____

7. Which colored bucket has the most creeper eggs? _____

8. Which two colored buckets, when combined, add up to 228 creeper eggs? _____ and _____

HARDCORE MODE: Try this hardcore math challenge!

9. What is the sum of all the creeper eggs? _____

EQUAL PARTS CHALLENGE

Use a ruler or the edge of a piece of paper to help you draw partitions in the shapes below.

When you partition something, you divide it into sections

1. The first gold ingot below is partitioned, or divided, into two equal parts with the red line.

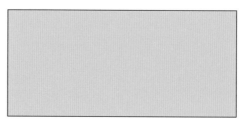

There is another way to divide this gold ingot into two equal, symmetrical parts.
Draw it below:

Use your pencil to shade in one of the pieces above.
What fraction describes this picture? _____

2. Partition the iron ingot into **3** equal shares in two different ways.

Use your pencil to shade in one of the pieces above.
What fraction describes this picture? _____

3. Partition the iron ingot into **4** equal shares in two different ways.

Use your pencil to shade in one of the pieces above.
What fraction describes this picture? _____

MYSTERY MESSAGE WITH MULTIPLICATION

Solve each multiplication equation below. Use the answers to solve the riddle.

1. $57 \times 9 = 513$

2. 72×5

3. 27×9

4. 57×6

5. 41×6

6. 46×8

A   G   Q   S   N   U

7. 84×4

8. 26×9

9. 50×7

10. 78×6

11. 41×8

E   C   D   I   R

Q: What is Steve's favorite type of dancing?

COPY THE LETTERS FROM THE ANSWERS ABOVE TO FIND OUT.

342   243   368   513   328   336

350   513   246   234   468   246   360

MULTIPLICATION AND DIVISION MYSTERY NUMBER

Some hacker has replaced a number from each of the below equations with a TNT block. Use multiplication and division to solve for the missing numbers.

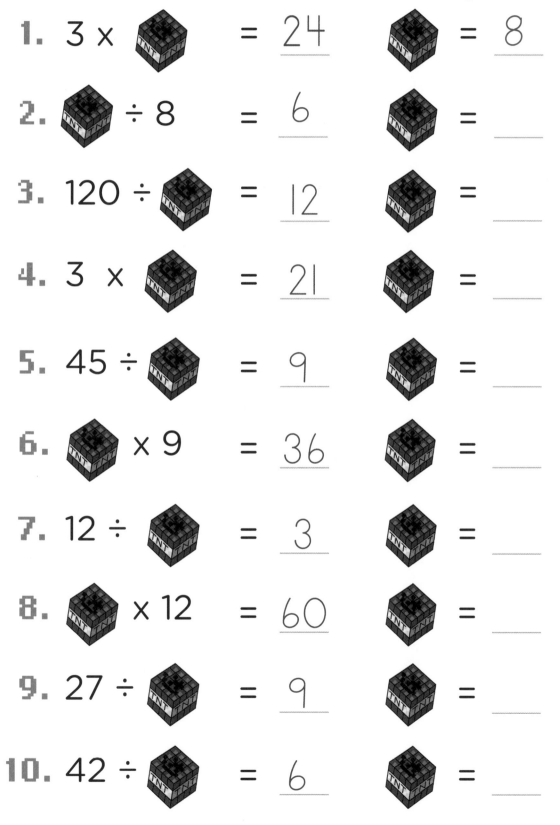

1. 3 x  = 24    = 8

2.  ÷ 8 = 6    = ____

3. 120 ÷  = 12    = ____

4. 3 x  = 21    = ____

5. 45 ÷  = 9    = ____

6.  x 9 = 36    = ____

7. 12 ÷  = 3    = ____

8.  x 12 = 60    = ____

9. 27 ÷  = 9    = ____

10. 42 ÷  = 6    = ____

SNOW GOLEM'S NUMBER CHALLENGE

Match the Snow Golem with the description of the number.

1. Hundreds: **1** Tens: **2** Ones: **9**

642÷2

2. Hundreds: **3** Tens: **2** Ones: **1**

51x8

3. Hundreds: **1** Tens: **7** Ones: **5**

26x9

4. Hundreds: **4** Tens: **0** Ones: **8**

875÷5

5. Hundreds: **2** Tens: **3** Ones: **4**

43 x 3

SKIP COUNT CHALLENGE

A rare but hostile chicken jockey is headed your way!
Count by 6 to escape.

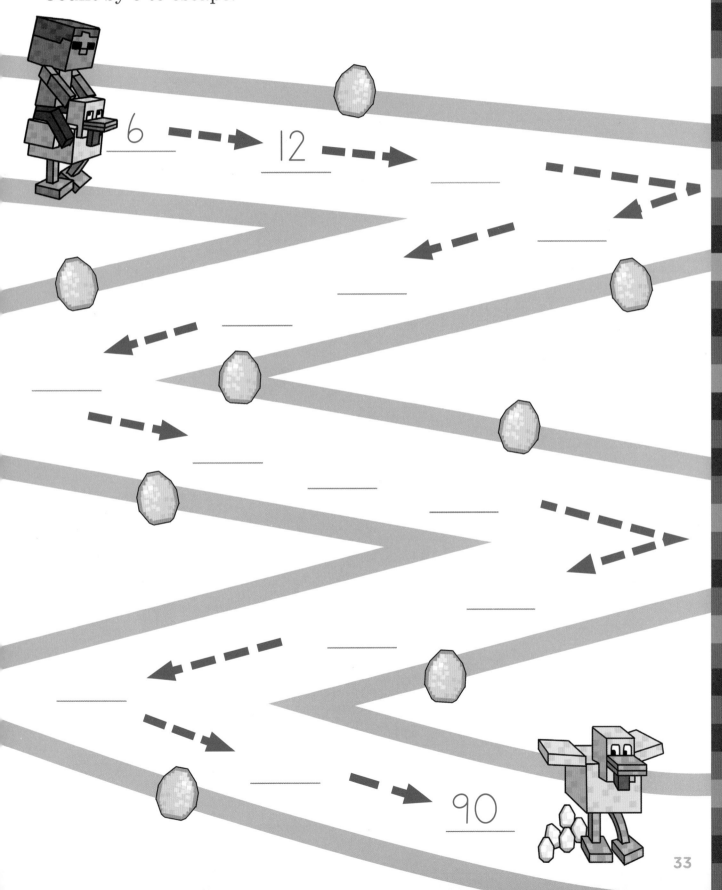

6 → 12 → ___ → ___

___ ← ___

___ → ___

___ → ___

___ ← ___

___ → 90

CREATING POTIONS

Use the recipes below to figure out the number of items needed to make more of each potion.

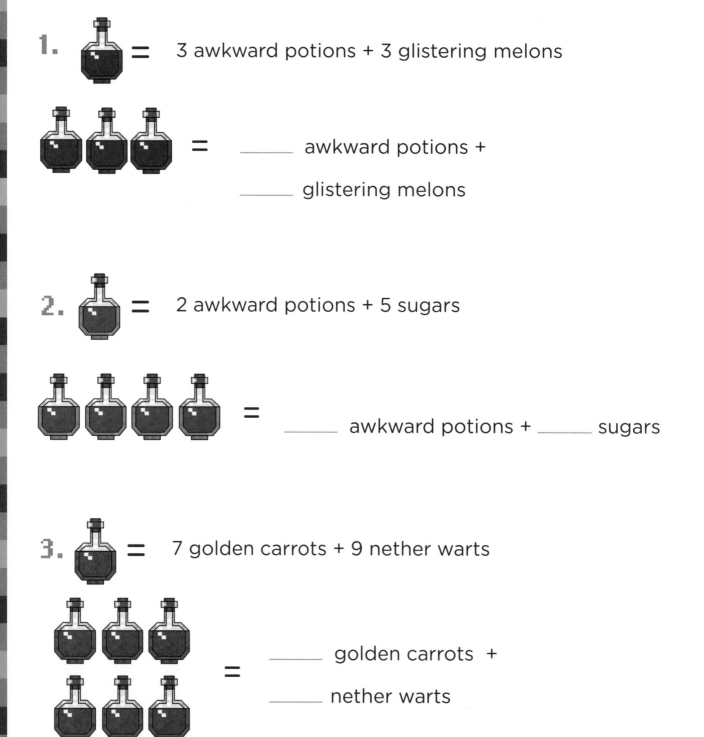

1. = 3 awkward potions + 3 glistering melons

= _____ awkward potions +

_____ glistering melons

2. = 2 awkward potions + 5 sugars

= _____ awkward potions + _____ sugars

3. = 7 golden carrots + 9 nether warts

= _____ golden carrots +

_____ nether warts

INVISIBILITY POTION FORMULA

4.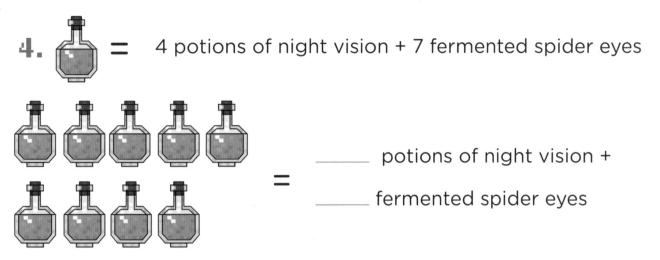

= 4 potions of night vision + 7 fermented spider eyes

= _____ potions of night vision +

_____ fermented spider eyes

INVISIBILITY POTION INGREDIENTS TABLE

Use the formula above to determine how much you need of each ingredient below. The first one is done for you.

Night Vision Potion	8			
Fermented Spider Eyes				

ADVENTURES IN GEOMETRY: PERIMETER AND AREA

Steve is building new rooms in his house. Multiply the number of blocks to help him find the perimeter and area of the walls.

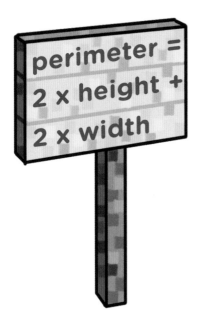

perimeter =
2 x height +
2 x width

1. Perimeter = _____

If Steve doubles the height of this wall,

what would the new perimeter be? _____

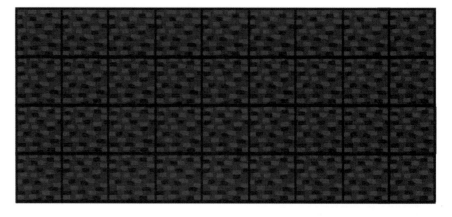

2. Perimeter = _____

If Steve destroys the right half of this wall,
what would the new perimeter be? _____

3. Perimeter = _____

Alex built a wall twice as wide as this one.
What was the perimeter of her new wall?

_____

**area =
height x
width**

4. Area = _____

If Steve doubles the height of this wall,
what would the new area be? _____

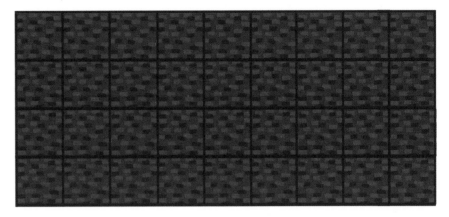

5. Area = _____

If Steve destroys the right half of this wall,
what would the new area be? _____

6. Area = _____

Alex built a wall twice as big as this one.
What was the area of her wall? _____

WORD PROBLEMS

Use multiplication and division to solve these word problems.

1. Alex is planning to get carrots for her horses. She has 32 horses and each horse needs 8 carrots a day. How many carrots does she need to feed the horses each day?

Answer: _____

2. Steve plants melon seeds in his garden. He figures out that 3 seeds make one melon. If his garden made 48 melons, how many seeds did he plant?

Answer: _____

3. You destroy 12 Endermen with your iron sword! If each Enderman drops 4 Ender pearls when he dies, how many pearls do you collect?

Answer: _____

4. Baby zombies are spawning! You spot 16 little green zombies total. If you encounter 3 more groups of 16 baby zombies, how many zombies will you encounter in all?

Answer: _____

5. Steve needs to feed his mooshrooms and baby mooshrooms. Each adult needs 2 wheat items, while each baby needs just 1 wheat item. If he has 12 adult mooshrooms and 5 baby mooshrooms, how many wheat items does he need to feed them?

Answer: _____

6. Escape the charged creepers! If it takes you 6 minutes to row your wooden boat 9 feet, how long do you estimate it will take you to row across a river that is 54 feet wide?

Answer: _____

7. Steve has 68 blocks of redstone that he needs to transport to his house. If 2 blocks can fit in his mining cart during each trip, how many trips will he have to take to move them all?

Answer: _____

8. You want to make cookies for all of your favorite players. You need 2 wheat items to make each batch of cookies. If you make 63 batches of cookies, how many wheat items do you need?

Answer: _____

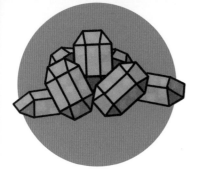

PLACE VALUE

Match the answer to each equation on the left with the number of emeralds on the right to help Steve calculate how many emeralds total he mined on a certain day.

1. 3 x 12 x 5 = _____

2. 9 x 22 x 4 = _____

3. 15 x 3 x 9 = _____

4. 7 x 14 x 6 = _____

5. 6 x 24 x 4 = _____

6. 2 x 35 x 9 = _____

7. 13 x 8 x 2 = _____

A   405

B   630

C   576

D   180

E   588

F   208

G   792

GHASTLY NUMBER CHALLENGE

Match the answer to the Ghast's equation on the right with the correct place value description on the left.

1. Hundreds: **9** Tens: **1** Ones: **2**

2. Hundreds: **6** Tens: **7** Ones: **2**

3. Hundreds: **3** Tens: **0** Ones: **8**

4. Hundreds: **2** Tens: **2** Ones: **0**

5. Hundreds: **7** Tens: **6** Ones: **0**

6. Hundreds: **2** Tens: **4** Ones: **9**

7. Hundreds: **5** Tens: **2** Ones: **0**

44 x 7

76 x 10

24 x 38

2200 ÷ 10

498 ÷ 2

42 x 16

26 x 20

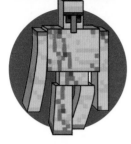

MOB MEASUREMENTS

Find out how many inches tall each mob is using multiplication and addition.

1 foot = 12 inches

Example:

1.

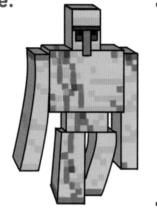

Iron Golem
3 feet, 4 inches

12 x 3 = <u>36</u> inches

36 + 4 = <u>40</u> inches tall

2.

Zombie
2 feet, 6 inches

Height in inches = _____

3.

Skeleton
3 feet, 1 inch

Height in inches = _____

4.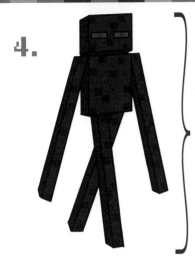

Enderman

4 feet, 3 inches

Height in inches = _____

5.

Rabbit

1 foot, 6 inches

Height in inches = _____

METRIC MEASUREMENTS

Complete the chart using the formula provided.

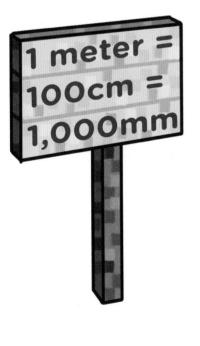

1 meter = 100cm = 1,000mm

	Length in meters	Length in cm	Length in mm
	2	200	2,000
		400	
	1.5		1,500
			2,500
	1		

ADVENTURES IN GEOMETRY

Identify the angle shown in each picture as acute, right, or obtuse.

obtuse   acute   right

1. _____

2. _____

3. _____

4. _____

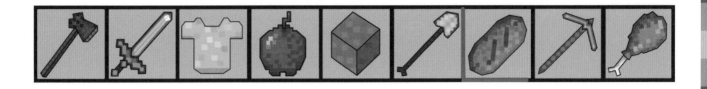

5. _____

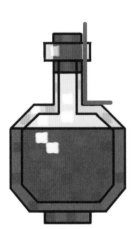

6. _____

7. _____

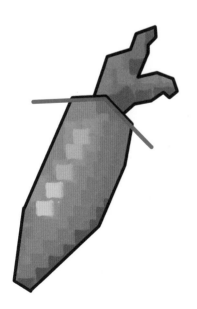

8. _____

9. _____

MULTIPLICATION AND DIVISION MYSTERY NUMBER

A troublesome creeper has replaced a number in each equation with a creeper spawn egg! Use multiplication and division to determine the missing number.

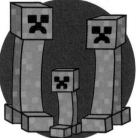

1. $217 \div$ $= 31$ $=$ _____

2. $\div 5 = 85$ $=$ _____

3. $548 \div 4 =$ $=$ _____

4. $424 \div$ $= 4$ $=$ _____

5. $48 \div 6 =$ $=$ _____

6. $\div 3 = 126$ $=$ _____

7. $72 \div$ $= 9$ $=$ _____

8. $512 \div 8 =$ $=$ _____

9. $9 \times$ $= 702$ $=$ _____

MYSTERY MESSAGE
WITH MULTIPLICATION AND DIVISION

Solve the multiplication and division problems below. Then write the letters in the blank spaces at the bottom of the page to get the answer to the joke!

1. $892 \div 2 =$ _____   G

2. $45 \times 8 =$ _____   B

3. $623 \div 7 =$ _____   I

4. $1122 \div 6 =$ _____   N

5. $91 \times 9 =$ _____   O

6. $230 \times 4 =$ _____   X

Q: What is a Minecrafter's favorite sport?

COPY THE LETTERS FROM THE ANSWERS ABOVE TO FIND OUT.

Answer:

_____ _____ _____ _____ _____ _____
360   819   920   89   187   446

ANSWER KEY

Page 6: Multiplication by Grouping
2. 4 x 4 = 16 cows
3. 3 x 7 = 21 chickens
4. 1 x 9 = 9 wolves
5. 6 x 4 = 24 sheep

Page 7: Mystery Message with Multiplication
2. 12
3. 18
4. 24
5. 35
6. 40
7. 16
8. 54
9. 30
Answer: He goes TO DAYSCARE

Page 8: Zombie's Guide to Place Value
2. 4,000 + 600 + 70 + 2
3. 2,000 + 700 + 90 + 8
4. 8,000 + 500 + 40 + 0
5. 3,000 + 100 + 50 + 1
6. 6,000 + 700 + 30 + 6
7. 5,000 + 400 + 50 + 9

Page 9: Math Facts Challenge
7, 14, 21, 28, 35, 42, 49, 56, 63, 70, 77, 84

Page 10: Telling Time
2. 4:40
3. 11:05
4. 9:20
5. 7:10
6. 4:50

Page 11: The Trading Table
1. 32 emeralds
2. 16 emeralds
3. 24 emeralds
4. 48 emeralds
5. The farmer and the butcher.
6. The librarian.
7. The farmer's collection.

Pages 12–13: Geometry Skills Practice
2. 3 x 6 = 18 potions
3. 4 x 4 = 16 experience orbs
4. 2 x 7 = 14 clocks
5. 3 x 7 = 21 creepers
6. 4 x 3 = 12 wolves
7. 1 x 9 = 9 zombies
8. 2 x 6 = 12 spiders
9. 3 x 5 = 15 cows
Hardcore mode: 7 x 7 = 49 + 5 = 54 experience orbs

Pages 14–15: Multiplication Word Problems
2. 6 buckets
3. 16 planks
4. 18 experience orbs
5. 42 blocks
6. 12 pieces
7. 100 minutes
8. 27 fish
9. 24 bottles

Page 16: Ghast's Guide to Place Value
2. 36, 40
3. 48, 50
4. 15, 20
5. 28, 30
6. 40, 40
7. 63, 60

Page 17: Math Facts Challenge
4, 8, 12, 16, 20, 24, 28, 32, 36, 40, 44, 48

Page 18: Minute Hand Mystery
2. 45 minutes

3. 15 minutes

4. 40 minutes

5. 55 minutes

6. 25 minutes

Page 19: Equal Trade

1. 10 pennies
2. 5 nickels
3. 15 pennies
4. 4 quarters
5. 5 dimes

Page 20: Adventures in Geometry

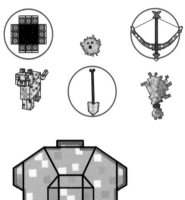

Page 21: Shelter Geometry

1. Area of Alex's wall

8 x 4 = 32

2. Area of Steve's wall

5 x 6 = 30

3. Alex's wall
4. 2 more blocks
5. 62

Page 22: Multiplication by Grouping

1. 3 x 3 = 9
2. 5 x 3 = 15
3. 6 x 3 = 18
4. 2 x 3 = 6
5. 4 x 3 = 12

Page 23: Mystery Message with Multiplication and Division

2. 102
3. 308
4. 62
5. 825
6. 231
7. 603
Answer: Herobrine

Page 24: Enderman's Guide to Place Value

2. E
3. F
4. A
5. C
6. G
7. D

Page 25: Skip Count Challenge

9, 18, 27, 36, 45, 54, 63, 72, 81, 90, 99, 108

Page 26: Telling Time

2. 7:55
3. 4:15
4. 9:20
5. 6:40
6. 12:05
7. 8:30
8. 5:10

Page 27: Spawn Egg Challenge

1. 135
2. 20
3. 188
4. 78
5. 40
6. 212
7. black
8. green and pink
9. 673

Pages 28–29: Equal Parts Challenge

1.

Fraction: ½

2.

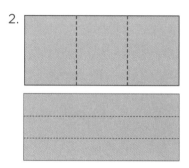

Fraction: ⅓

3.

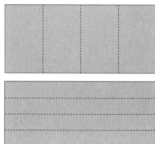

Fraction: ¼

Page 30: Mystery Message with Multiplication

2. 360

3. 243

4. 342

5. 246

6. 368

7. 336

8. 234

9. 350

10. 468

11. 328

Answer: Square Dancing

Page 31: Multiplication and Division Mystery Number

2. 48	3. 10	4. 7	5. 5	6. 4
7. 4	8. 5	9. 3	10. 7	

Page 32: Snow Golem's Number Challenge

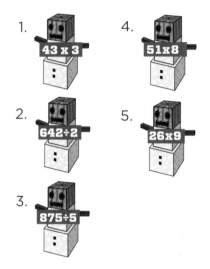

1. 43 x 3
2. 642÷2
3. 875÷5
4. 51x8
5. 26x9

Page 33: Skip Count Challenge

6, 12, 18, 24, 30, 36, 42, 48, 54, 60, 66, 72, 78, 84, 90

Pages 34–35: Creating Potions

1. 9, 9

2. 8, 20

3. 42, 54

4. 36, 63

Night Vision Potion	8	12	16	20
Fermented Spider Eyes	14	21	28	35

Pages 36–37: Adventures in Geometry: Perimeter and Area

1. Current perimeter: 26
   New perimeter: 34
2. Current perimeter: 22
   New perimeter: 16
3. Current perimeter: 18
   New perimeter: 26
4. Current area: 36
   New area: 72
5. Current area: 30
   New area: 15
6. Current area: 20
   New area: 40

Pages 38–39: Word Problems

1. 256 carrots
2. 144 seeds
3. 48 pearls
4. 64 baby zombies
5. 29 wheat items
6. 36 minutes
7. 34 trips
8. 126 wheat items

Page 40: Place Value

1. 180 (D)   2. 792 (G)
3. 405 (A)   4. 588 (E)
5. 576 (C)   6. 630 (B)
7. 208 (F)

Page 41: Ghastly Number Challenge

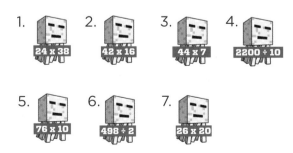

1. 24 x 38
2. 42 x 16
3. 44 x 7
4. 2200 ÷ 10
5. 76 x 10
6. 498 ÷ 2
7. 26 x 20

Pages 42–43: Mob Measurements

2. 30 inches
3. 37 inches
4. 51 inches
5. 18 inches

	Length in meters	Length in cm	Length in mm
	2	200	2,000
	4	400	4,000
	1.5	150	1,500
	2.5	250	2,500
	1	100	1,000

Pages 44–45: Adventures in Geometry

1. clock: obtuse
2. shovel: obtuse
3. ghast: acute
4. chicken: obtuse
5. inventory bar: right
6. potion: right
7. bow and arrow: acute
8. carrot: obtuse
9. pickaxe: acute

Page 46: Multiplication and Division Mystery Number

1. 7   2. 425   3. 137
4. 106   5. 8   6. 378
7. 8   8. 64   9. 78

Page 47: Mystery Message with Multiplication and Division

1. 446
2. 360
3. 89
4. 187
5. 819
6. 920
Answer: boxing

MATH FOR MINECRAFTERS

WORD PROBLEMS

MULTIPLYING ONE-DIGIT NUMBERS

Read the problem carefully. Use the pictures (or draw your own) for extra help. Write the answer in the space provided.

1. You meet 8 skeletons and each one shoots 7 arrows at you. How many arrows are shot in all?

2. You are attacked by 6 groups of 4 silverfish. How many silverfish are attacking in all?

3. A ghast shoots 10 fireballs at you. A group of 3 more ghasts approaches and each ghast shoots 2 fireballs at you. How many fireballs are shot at you in all?

4. You see 10 creepers. You get 3 unit of gunpowder from each of them. How many unit of gunpowder do you get in all?

5. You find 7 shulkers in an End temple. You take 4 damage from each of them. How much damage do you take in all?

6. You place 3 torches on each of 3 cave walls. How many torches do you place?

7. You brew 4 potions of Leaping and each one restores 2 hearts. How many hearts can be restored with 8 potions of Leaping?

8. You start your game with 9 shovels in your inventory. You have 3 times as many swords in your inventory. How many swords do you have?

MULTIPLYING ONE-DIGIT NUMBERS

(continued from previous page)

9. You encounter 6 groups of 7 cave spiders. How many spiders do you encounter?

10. You destroy a bunch of zombies and collect 5 pieces of rotten flesh. If you collect this much rotten flesh 3 times in one day, how many pieces of rotten flesh do you collect in all?

11. To make one golden sword, you need 2 gold ingots. If you want to make 8 golden swords, how many gold ingots do you need?

12. You find 7 chests in each of 3 caves that you explore. How many chests do you find in all?

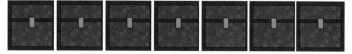

13. You make 3 towers. Each one is made of 10 blocks of obsidian. How many obsidian blocks do you use in all?

14. You stack 4 rows of 5 redstone ore blocks to build a wall. How many redstone ore blocks do you use in all?

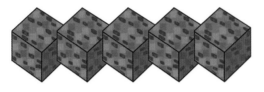

15. A group of 4 skeletons attacks you. Each skeleton shoots 8 arrows at you. How many arrows do the skeletons shoot in all?

HARDCORE MODE

Steve, Alex, and a villager collect as many emeralds as possible. Steve only collects 3 emeralds. The villager collects 4 times as many emeralds as Steve. Alex collects the most. She collects 6 times as many emeralds as the villager.

How many emeralds does Alex collect?

PVP SHOWDOWN

Which player earned the most experience points today? Solve the equations in each column then add up the answers to determine the winner of this PVP showdown.

1. $7 \times 6 =$ $6 \times 8 =$

2. $3 \times 5 =$ $4 \times 9 =$

3. $8 \times 4 =$ $6 \times 2 =$

4. $9 \times 1 =$ $3 \times 3 =$

5. $4 \times 7 =$ $9 \times 6 =$

6. $6 \times 6 =$ $3 \times 8 =$

TOTAL POINTS   _____   _____

Circle the winner:

 ALEX    STEVE

MULTIPLYING ONE- AND TWO-DIGIT NUMBERS

Read the problem carefully. Use the pictures (or draw your own) for extra help. Write the answer in the space provided.

1. You use 20 blocks of cobblestone to build a tower. How many blocks of cobblestone do you use to build 4 towers?

2. A player rides in the railcart 15 times a day. After 3 days, how many times does the player ride in the railcart?

3. There are 14 blacksmith villagers who have 3 emeralds each. How many emeralds do the Blacksmith villagers have in all?

4.

You tame 2 wolves a day for 16 days. How many wolves do you tame in all?

MULTIPLYING ONE- AND TWO-DIGIT NUMBERS

(continued from previous page)

5. You have 4 farms with 17 sheep on each farm. How many sheep do you have in all?

6. 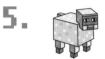 You get 11 experience points from every creeper you kill. You kill 4 creepers. How many experience points do you get?

7. You mine 8 blocks of granite for 16 mornings straight. How many blocks do you mine in all?

8. You destroy 3 times more Endermen than zombie pigmen. You destroy 25 zombie pigmen. How many Endermen do you destroy?

9. Seven witches throw 26 splash potions in a day. How many splash potions do the witches throw in all?

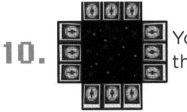 **10.** You see 4 groups of 16 Endermen when you enter the End. How many Endermen do you see in all?

11. You tame 5 ocelots every time you enter the Jungle Biome. You enter the Jungle Biome 32 times. How many ocelots do you tame?

12. 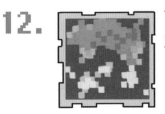 You use a map 8 times every time you play. If you play 22 times, how many times do you use a map?

MULTIPLYING ONE- AND TWO-DIGIT NUMBERS

(continued from previous page)

13.  You need 3 lapis lazuli to craft each enchanted bow and arrow. How many lapis lazuli do you need to make 19 enchanted bow and arrows?

14. 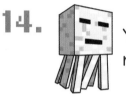 You destroy 15 ghasts in 8 minutes. If you continue at that rate, how many ghasts will you destroy in 24 minutes?

15.  A skeleton shoots 7 arrows at each villager he sees. He sees 29 villagers. How many arrows does he shoot?

HARDCORE MODE

There are 14 desert temples. Each one has 10 active traps. You deactivate 14 of the traps by breaking the pressure plate. How many active traps are left?

PVP SHOWDOWN

Which player earned the most experience points today? Solve the equations in each column then add up the answers to determine the winner of this PVP showdown.

1.	12 x 6 =	10 x 8 =
2.	3 x 50 =	14 x 9 =
3.	11 x 4 =	16 x 2 =
4.	19 x 1 =	3 x 13 =
5.	24 x 2 =	15 x 6 =
6.	6 x 13 =	12 x 8 =

TOTAL POINTS _____ _____

Circle the winner:

ALEX   STEVE

DIVISION WITH 1- AND 2-DIGIT NUMBERS

Read the problem carefully. Use the pictures for extra help. Write the answer in the space provided.

1. You catch 9 fish with your fishing rod. You divide the fish among 3 cats. How many fish does each cat get?

2. There are 8 bats in 4 dungeons. If each dungeon has the same number of bats, how many bats are in each one?

3. There are 6 villagers. If each house in the village can fit 3 villagers, how many houses do they need?

4.  You have 4 diamond swords. You store 1 sword in each chest you own. How many chests do you own?

5. You have 15 skeleton spawn eggs. You sort them into 5 equal groups. How many eggs are in each group?

6. You make 3 identical walls out of 12 blocks of sandstone. How many blocks of sandstone do you use for each wall?

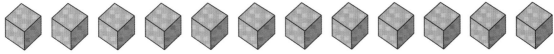

7. You have 18 diamonds. You give 6 of them to each villager you see until you're all out of diamonds. How many villagers did you see?

8. You have 16 blocks of wool in 4 different colors: blue, pink, lime, and yellow. If you have the same amount of every color, how many blocks do you have in each color?

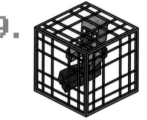

9. You approach a monster spawner in an Overworld dungeon. It spawns 20 monsters in all. If it spawns 5 of each kind of monster, how many kinds of monsters does it spawn?

10. You have 12 Ender eye pearls in your inventory. You place an equal amount in two different chests. How many Ender eye pearls do you place in each chest?

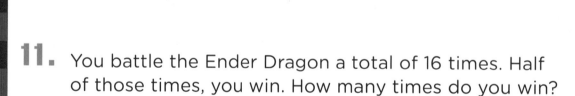

11. You battle the Ender Dragon a total of 16 times. Half of those times, you win. How many times do you win?

12. You earn 24 experience orbs for destroying a group of zombies. If every zombie you destroy earns you 6 experience orbs, how many zombies did you destroy?

13. You start your game with 20 bones. You need 2 bones to tame every wolf. How many wolves can you tame?

14. You battle 24 ghasts in the Nether. If you destroy 3 ghasts a minute, how many minutes does it take to destroy all of the ghasts?

15. A player has 10 hearts. He loses 1 heart every time he runs into a zombie. How many zombies can he run into before he's out of hearts?

HARDCORE MODE

You craft 27 tools and 6 pieces of armor. You place all of these items in 3 different chests for safe keeping. If you have an equal amount of items in all 3 chests, how many items are stored in each chest?

PVP SHOWDOWN

Which player earned the most experience points today? Solve the equations in each column then add up the answers to determine the winner of this PVP showdown.

1. 12 ÷ 6 =   16 ÷ 8 =

2. 15 ÷ 3 =   9 ÷ 3 =

3. 12 ÷ 4 =   18 ÷ 2 =

4. 20 ÷ 5 =   14 ÷ 7 =

5. 49 ÷ 7 =   42 ÷ 6 =

6. 16 ÷ 4 =   18 ÷ 3 =

TOTAL POINTS _____   _____

Circle the winner:

 ALEX    STEVE

DIVISION WITH 1- AND 2-DIGIT NUMBERS

(continued)

1. You need 12 Eyes of Ender to activate an End portal. You get 4 Eyes of Ender from every villager you trade with. How many villagers do you need to trade with to have enough Eyes of Ender to activate the End portal?

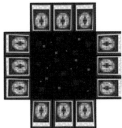

2. If each bowl of mushroom stew restores 2 hunger points, how many bowls do you need to eat to restore 24 hunger points?

3. If every snow golem drops 8 snowballs when destroyed, how many snow golems must be destroyed to get 64 snowballs?

4. If you can craft 9 boats a week using your resources, how many weeks will it take to craft 27 boats?

DIVISION WITH 1- AND 2-DIGIT NUMBERS

(continued from previous page)

5.  There are 63 apples in your inventory today. Each horse on your farm needs to be fed 7 apples. How many horses can you feed?

6. To brew 4 potions of Water Breathing, you need 32 pufferfish. How many pufferfish do you need to make 1 potion of Water Breathing?

7. 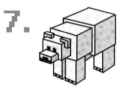 Every polar bear drops 6 fish when destroyed. If you need 36 fish, how many polar bears do you need to destroy?

8. You craft 5 Jack o' Lanterns every day. If you have 35 Jack o' Lanterns, how many days did you spend crafting them?

9.  Your farm has 42 cows. You divide them equally among 7 farms. How many cows do you keep on each farm?

10.  You encounter 54 creepers. You destroy 9 of them with each block of TNT you use. How many TNT blocks do you need to destroy all of the creepers?

11.  It takes you 81 minutes to craft 9 houses. How many minutes would you estimate it takes to craft each house?

12.  Your cobblestone house has 20 windows. It has the same number of windows on all 4 walls of the house. How many windows does it have on each wall?

DIVISION WITH 1- AND 2-DIGIT NUMBERS

(continued from previous page)

13. Every time you enter the Nether fortress, you battle 3 wither skeletons. If you battle 36 wither skeletons, how many times did you enter the Nether fortress?

14. You place 8 rows of grass blocks. You use 32 grass blocks in all. How many grass blocks did you place in each row?

15. You use your enchantment table to enchant 56 swords and shovels. You enchant 7 items at a time. How many groups of items do you enchant?

HARDCORE MODE

A group of blazes in the Nether fortress shoots 54 fireballs at you. You dodge all of them. Another group of blazes shoot an additional 21 fireballs at you. You are hit by 12 of them. If each blaze can only shoot 3 fireballs, how many blazes did you battle?

PVP SHOWDOWN

Which player earned the most experience points today? Solve the equations in each column then add up the answers to determine the winner of this PVP showdown.

	Alex	Steve
1.	81 ÷ 9 =	64 ÷ 8 =
2.	30 ÷ 5 =	24 ÷ 4 =
3.	92 ÷ 4 =	60 ÷ 5 =
4.	36 ÷ 2 =	56 ÷ 8 =
5.	40 ÷ 8 =	42 ÷ 6 =
6.	21 ÷ 3 =	55 ÷ 11 =

TOTAL POINTS _____   _____

Circle the winner:

 ALEX    STEVE

DIVISION WITH 1- AND 2-DIGIT NUMBERS

Read the problem carefully. Use the pictures for extra help. Write the answer in the space provided.

1.  You start a game with 34 hunger points. Every time you build a shelter, you lose 2 hunger points. How many shelters can you build before you lose all of your hunger points?

2. You swing your sword 68 times, but it takes 17 swings to destroy each zombie. How many zombies can you destroy?

3.  Your wolves destroy a total of 64 creepers in the Overworld. If each of your wolves destroyed 4 creepers, how many wolves do you have?

4.  Squids drop 72 ink sacs into the water. You dive down to collect them, but you have to come up for air every time you collect 8 ink sacs. How many times do you come up for air as you collect all of the ink sacs?

5. You have 85 minutes until nightfall. It takes you 5 minutes to build a shelter. How many shelters can you build before nightfall?

6. You have 49 empty buckets. You put them into groups of 7 to fill with milk. How many groups of buckets do you have?

7. There are 90 ocelots in the Jungle Biome. A group of 5 ocelots is enough to scare away 1 creeper. How many creepers can all of the ocelots scare away?

8.  You want to craft 2 equally sized beacons using 56 blocks. How many blocks will you use for each beacon?

DIVIDING 1- AND 2-DIGIT NUMBERS

(continued from previous page)

9. You use 95 arrows to destroy a group of cave spiders. If it takes 5 arrows to destroy 1 cave spider, how many cave spiders were there in the group?

10. A group of creepers drops 44 units of gunpowder. Each creeper drops 2 units of gunpowder. How many creepers are in the group?

11. You find 76 cobwebs in an abandoned mineshaft. With each snip of your shears, you collect 4 cobwebs. How many snips does it take to collect all of the cobwebs?

12. A group of zombie pigmen drops 63 pieces of rotten flesh. If each zombie pigman drops 3 pieces of rotten flesh, how many zombie pigman are in the group?

13. A ghast hurls 81 fireballs at you and hits you every time. You die and respawn after being hit by 9 of them. How many times do you die and respawn?

14. You have 75 spawn eggs in your inventory. You use 15 of them every time you play. How many times do you play before running out of spawn eggs?

15. You are trying to build a 54-step staircase out of sandstone blocks. You stop after every 9 blocks to rest and eat something. How many times do you stop?

HARDCORE MODE

If each of a wither's 3 heads spit 18 skulls at you during a battle and you take damage every time 6 skulls are spit at you, how many times do you take damage?

PVP SHOWDOWN

Which player earned the most experience points today? Solve the equations in each column then add up the answers to determine the winner of this PVP showdown.

1.	$96 \div 6 =$	$76 \div 2 =$
2.	$45 \div 5 =$	$44 \div 11 =$
3.	$68 \div 4 =$	$16 \div 2 =$
4.	$9 \div 1 =$	$33 \div 3 =$
5.	$14 \div 7 =$	$81 \div 9 =$
6.	$64 \div 2 =$	$21 \div 7 =$

TOTAL POINTS _____   _____

Circle the winner:

 ALEX    STEVE

MULTIPLYING AND DIVIDING WITHIN 100

Read the problem carefully. Use the pictures (or draw your own) for extra help. Write the answer in the space provided.

1.  You ride the minecart rail 2 times a day for 34 days. How many times do you ride the minecart rail?

2. You want to transport 36 chests to your base, but you can only transport 4 chests at a time. How many times do you need to transport groups of chests?

3.  You visit the Desert Biome 12 times more often than the Jungle Biome. If you visit the Jungle Biome 3 times, how many times do you visit the Desert Biome?

4. You have 49 splash potions. You need 7 splash potions to cure each zombie villager. How many zombie villagers can you cure?

MULTIPLYING AND DIVIDING WITHIN 100

(continued from previous page)

5. You use your new saddle to ride 7 groups of 6 pigs. How many pigs do you ride in all?

6.  You collect 76 pieces of raw beef after destroying a group of mooshrooms. If each mooshroom drops 4 pieces of raw beef, how many mooshrooms did you destroy?

7. You drink 4 potions of Swiftness and 8 times as many potions of Strength. How many potions of Strength did you drink?

8.  You visit the End 55 times. Every 5 times you visit, you find Elytra! How many times do you find Elytra?

9. 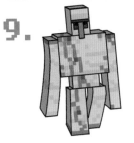 An iron golem drops 35 red flowers. A group of 7 villagers divides the flowers equally among themselves. How many flowers does each villager get?

10. 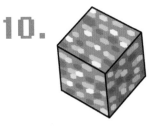 You want to mine 60 layers of diamond ore. If your pickaxe breaks after every 12 layers, how many times does your pickaxe break?

11.  You place 12 rows of 7 lapis lazuli ore blocks. How many lapis lazuli ore blocks do you place in all?

12. 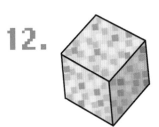 You place 30 iron blocks in 6 equal rows. How many iron blocks are in each row?

MULTIPLYING AND DIVIDING WITHIN 100

(continued from previous page)

13. You gather 21 ingredients to make a potion. You need 3 ingredients to make each bottle of potion. How many bottles of potion can you make?

14. You chop down a total of 63 trees. You build 7 beds from all of the wood. How many trees make a bed?

15. You destroy 10 mobs in one day in Survival mode. You destroy 8 times as many mobs the next day. How many mobs do you destroy the next day?

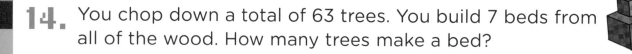

HARDCORE MODE

You want to make 23 cakes. Each one requires 3 milk and 2 sugar. You have 64 milk and 40 sugar. How much more do you need of each ingredient?

PVP SHOWDOWN

Which player earned the most experience points today? Solve the equations in each column then add up the answers to determine the winner of this PVP showdown.

1.	27 ÷ 3 =	8 x 1 =
2.	45 ÷ 5 =	4 x 3 =
3.	8 x 5 =	6 ÷ 2 =
4.	14 ÷ 2 =	21 ÷ 3 =
5.	34 ÷ 17 =	3 x 9 =
6.	6 x 4 =	42 ÷ 6 =

TOTAL POINTS _____   _____

Circle the winner:

ALEX   STEVE

MIXED OPERATIONS

Read the problem carefully. Write the answer in the space provided.

1. 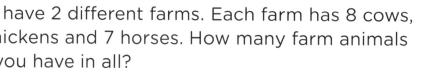 You craft 2 brewing stands, 5 beds, and 4 firework rockets each day for 2 days. How many items do you create in all?

2. 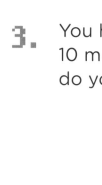 Over 4 days, you destroy 6 hostile mobs and 2 neutral mobs. If you destroy the same number of mobs each day, how many mobs do you destroy each day?

3. You have 4 diamonds in each of 8 chests. You collect 10 more diamonds while mining. How many diamonds do you have in all?

4.  You have 2 different farms. Each farm has 8 cows, 3 chickens and 7 horses. How many farm animals do you have in all?

5. There are 7 groups of 4 zombies approaching you. You destroy 16 zombies. How many zombies are left?

6.  You offer 9 emeralds to the first 3 villagers you meet and 6 emeralds to the next 4 villagers. How many emeralds do you offer for trade?

7. You build 8 beacons every day for 3 days. You build 12 beacons the next day. How many beacons do you build in all?

8. 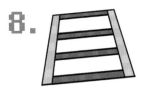 You place 8 minecart rails in the morning and 5 times that amount in the afternoon. Creepers blow up half of the rails. How many rails are left?

MIXED OPERATIONS

(continued from previous page)

9. You battle 8 skeletons and 4 zombies one day and 2 groups of 3 creepers the next day. How many mobs do you battle in all?

10.  You enchant 13 books and 4 swords every day for 2 days. You break 2 of the swords. How many enchanted items do you still have?

11. You shoot 7 arrows at a creeper and twice as many arrows at a giant zombie. Only 7 of them hit their target. How many arrows do not hit their target?

12. You see 6 groups of 5 creepers approaching. Before they get near you, 4 creepers explode. How many creepers are left?

13. Two witches each throw 3 potions of Slowness, 9 potions of Weakness, and 2 potions of Poison. How many potions are thrown in all?

14. You tame 7 groups of 5 ocelots and 3 groups of 6 horses. How many animals do you tame in all?

15. The Ender Dragon fires 4 Ender charges at you every time you enter the End. You enter the End 16 times one day and 5 times the next. How many Ender charges does the Ender Dragon fire in all?

HARDCORE MODE

You battle 16 ghasts and destroy half of them. The ones you destroy drop a variety of items. Half of them drop 2 gunpowder and the other half drop one ghast tear. How many items are dropped in all?

PVP SHOWDOWN

Which player earned the most experience points today? Solve the equations in each column then add up the answers to determine the winner of this PVP showdown.

1.	$18 \div 9 =$	$6 + 8 =$
2.	$7 - 5 =$	$4 \times 4 =$
3.	$9 + 4 =$	$6 \div 2 =$
4.	$5 \times 1 =$	$3 - 3 =$
5.	$8 \times 7 =$	$9 + 6 =$
6.	$16 \div 4 =$	$3 \times 8 =$

TOTAL POINTS _____ _____

Circle the winner:

 ALEX

 STEVE

DIVISION WITH REMAINDERS

Read the problem carefully. Use the pictures (or draw your own) for extra help. Write the answer in the space provided.

1. You have 43 experience points. You need 4 experience points to enchant a bow and arrow. How many bow and arrows can you enchant, and how many experience points will you have left over?

2.  You have 27 lily pads. You need 4 lily pads to help you cross each river. How many rivers can you cross with your lily pads and how many will be left over?

3. You plant 18 cactus blocks on your farm in rows of 5. How many rows do you plant, and how many blocks are left over?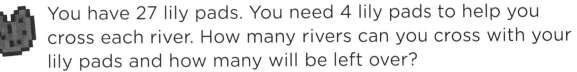

4. You place 35 items in equal amounts in 4 different chests. How many items are in each chest and how many are left over?

DIVISION WITH REMAINDERS

(continued from previous page)

5. You trade with 7 different villagers in 44 minutes. If it takes the same amount of time to trade with each villager, how much time do you spend trading with each villager? How much time is left over after you've traded with all of them?

6. You have 67 snowballs and want to make as many snow golems as you can. You need 8 snowballs to make every snow golem. How many snow golems can you make, and how many snowballs will you have left over?

7. 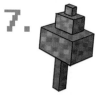 It takes 6 swings of your axe to chop down every spruce tree. If you only have enough durability to swing your axe 58 times, how many trees can you chop down, and how many swings could you still take?

8. You collect 87 Ender pearls after battling a group of Endermen. You need 4 Ender pearls to make one Eye of Ender. How many Eyes of Ender can you make, and how many Ender pearls will be left over?

MULTIPLICATION AND DIVISION OF 2- AND 3-DIGIT NUMBERS

Read the problem carefully. Use the pictures (or draw your own) for extra help. Write the answer in the space provided.

1. 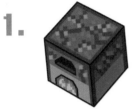 You have 27 coal blocks to use in your furnace. If each block of coal can smelt 80 items, how many items can you smelt?

2. 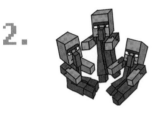 You have 150 zombie eggs in your inventory. You use 15 of those eggs every day to spawn zombies. How many days pass before you run out of zombie eggs?

3.  You lose 18 hunger points from exhaustion every day over 23 days of mining. How many hunger points do you lose over all 23 days?

4.  You brew 217 potions of Weakness. You need 7 potions to heal every zombie villager you meet. How many zombie villagers can you heal?

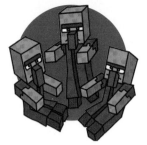

MULTIPLICATION AND DIVISION OF 2- AND 3-DIGIT NUMBERS

(continued from previous page)

5. You get 230 experience points from battling 5 skeletons. How many experience points do you estimate you get for battling each skeleton?

6. You have 196 wood planks. You need 7 wood planks to craft a boat. How many boats can you craft from all of your wood planks?

7. There are 122 donkeys total in the Plains Biome. If you bred them and tripled the number of donkeys in the Plains Biome, how many donkeys would there be?

HARDCORE MODE

Your dad says you can have 35 minutes of gaming time on every school day and 45 minutes of gaming time on each weekend day. Your mom says you can have 25 minutes of gaming time on every school day and 60 minutes on each weekend day. Which parent is offering you the most gaming time per week?

PVP SHOWDOWN

Which player earned the most experience points today? Solve the equations in each column then add up the answers to determine the winner of this PVP showdown.

1. $425 \div 5 =$ $126 \div 6 =$

2. $315 \div 5 =$ $44 \div 4 =$

3. $28 \times 2 =$ $62 \div 2 =$

4. $8 \times 2 =$ $42 \div 6 =$

5. $14 \div 7 =$ $19 \div 1 =$

6. $16 \times 6 =$ $3 \times 44 =$

TOTAL POINTS   _____   _____

Circle the winner:

ALEX   STEVE

ADDING AND SUBTRACTING FRACTIONS

Solve the equations and simplify your answers.

1.  You are attacked by a group of Endermen. You destroy ¼ of them with your sword and ²⁄₄ of them with your bow and arrow. What fraction of the Endermen did you destroy?

2. You battle a group of ghasts in the Nether. While you're battling, ¹⁄₆ of their fireballs miss you and ⁴⁄₆ of them are deflected by your shield. The rest inflict damage. What fraction of fireballs inflict damage?

3. You build ⁴⁄₈ of your cobblestone structure one day and ²⁄₈ of it the next day. What fraction of your cobblestone structure have you built in all?

4.  You use golden apples to cure ¹⁄₁₆ of a group of zombie villagers. You craft a few more golden apples and cure another ⁴⁄₁₆ of the zombie villagers. What fraction of villagers have not been cured?

5. An iron golem destroys $\frac{1}{12}$ of a group of zombies. You destroy $\frac{3}{12}$ of the zombies. What fraction of the zombies are destroyed?

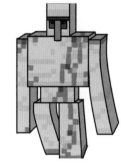

6. You use $\frac{3}{9}$ of your weapons in battle and $\frac{1}{9}$ of your weapons to mine valuable resources. What fraction of your weapons are still unused?

7. You use your brewing stand to brew a bunch of potions. You use $\frac{1}{5}$ of the potions on blazes, $\frac{1}{5}$ on wither skeletons, and $\frac{1}{5}$ on zombie pigmen. What fraction of your potions do you use?

8. You enchant your armor for added protection. You enchant $\frac{3}{7}$ of your armor the first day and $\frac{3}{7}$ of your armor the next day. What fraction of your armor is not enchanted?

ADDING AND SUBTRACTING FRACTIONS WITH DIFFERENT DENOMINATORS

Make the fractions equivalent. Then add them or subtract them. Simplify your answers.

1. You battle a group of hostile mobs. If $\frac{1}{6}$ of the hostile mobs fall in a lava pit and $\frac{3}{12}$ are destroyed by your arrows, what fraction of hostile mobs remain?

2. You use $\frac{1}{9}$ of your gold ingots to make a clock and $\frac{2}{3}$ of your gold ingots to make weapons. What fraction of your gold ingots do you use in all?

3. You use $\frac{1}{4}$ of your wooden sticks to make garden hoes. You use $\frac{1}{3}$ of your wooden sticks to make arrows. What fraction of your wooden sticks remains?

4.  You battle the Wither often, but you lose $\frac{3}{5}$ of the times and run away $\frac{2}{6}$ of the times. The rest of the times, you win. What fraction of your battles do you win?

5.  You used ⁴/₇ of your diamonds to make armor and ¹/₃ of them to make weapons. What fraction of your diamonds did you use in all?

6. Your inventory is getting full. You know that ¹/₅ of your inventory is food, ¹/₄ of it is tools, and ¹/₂₀ of it is building materials. What fraction of your inventory is none of these things?

7. If you eat ⁴/₁₀ of your fish and use ²/₅ of your fish to tame ocelots, what fraction of your fish do you use in all?

HARDCORE MODE

Write your own word problem with fractions below and show it to your friend, your teacher, or your parent. Challenge him or her to solve it!

_____

_____

_____

_____

PVP SHOWDOWN

Which player earned the most experience points today? Solve the equations in each column then add up the answers to determine the winner of this PVP showdown.

1. $\frac{1}{8} + \frac{2}{8} =$ $\frac{1}{6} + \frac{2}{6} =$

2. $\frac{1}{4} + \frac{1}{4} =$ $\frac{3}{6} + \frac{2}{6} =$

3. $\frac{3}{8} + \frac{4}{8} =$ $\frac{2}{6} + \frac{2}{6} =$

4. $\frac{3}{8} + \frac{1}{8} =$ $\frac{1}{3} + \frac{1}{3} =$

5. $\frac{4}{4} + \frac{6}{4} =$ $\frac{9}{6} + \frac{8}{6} =$

TOTAL POINTS   _____   _____

Circle the winner:

 **ALEX**    **STEVE**

ANSWER KEY

PAGE 54
1. 56 arrows
2. 24 silverfish
3. 16 fireballs
4. 30 unit of gunpowder

PAGE 55
5. 28 damage
6. 9 torches
7. 16 hearts
8. 27 swords

PAGE 56
9. 42 spiders
10. 15 pieces of rotten flesh
11. 16 gold ingots
12. 21 chests

PAGE 57
13. 30 obsidian blocks
14. 20 redstone ore blocks
15. 32 arrows

Hardcore mode
72 emeralds

PAGE 58
PVP Showdown
Alex: 162 experience points
Steve: 183 experience points

PAGE 59
1. 80 blocks
2. 45 times
3. 42 emeralds
4. 32 wolves

PAGE 60
5. 68 sheep
6. 44 experience points
7. 128 blocks
8. 75 Endermen

PAGE 61
9. 182 splash potions
10. 64 Endermen
11. 160 ocelots
12. 176 times

PAGE 62
13. 57 lapis lazuli
14. 45 ghasts
15. 203 arrows

Hardcore mode
126 active traps

PAGE 63
PVP Showdown
Alex: 411 experience points
Steve: 463 experience points

PAGE 64
1. 3 fish
2. 2 bats
3. 2 houses
4. 4 chests

PAGE 65
5. 3 eggs
6. 4 blocks
7. 3 villagers
8. 4 blocks

PAGE 66
9. 4 kinds
10. 6 Ender eye pearls
11. 8 times
12. 4 zombies

PAGE 67
13. 10 wolves
14. 8 minutes
15. 10 zombies

Hardcore mode
11 items

PAGE 68

PVP Showdown

Alex: 25 experience points

Steve: 29 experience points

PAGE 69

1. 3 villagers
2. 12 bowls
3. 8 snow golems
4. 3 weeks

PAGE 70

5. 9 horses
6. 8 pufferfish
7. 6 polar bears
8. 7 days

PAGE 71

9. 6 cows
10. 6 blocks
11. 9 minutes
12. 5 windows

PAGE 72

13. 12 times
14. 4 grass blocks
15. 8 groups of items

Hardcore mode

25 blazes

PAGE 73

PVP Showdown

Alex: 68 experience points

Steve: 45 experience points

PAGE 74

1. 17 shelters
2. 4 zombies
3. 16 tamed wolves
4. 9 times

PAGE 75

5. 17 shelters
6. 7 groups
7. 18 creepers
8. 28 blocks

PAGE 76

9. 19 cave spiders
10. 22 creepers
11. 19 snips
12. 21 zombie pigmen

PAGE 77

13. 9 times
14. 5 times
15. 6 times

Hardcore mode

9 times

PAGE 78

PVP Showdown

Alex: 85

Steve: 73

PAGE 79

1. 68 times
2. 9 times
3. 36 times
4. 7 zombie villagers

PAGE 80

5. 42 pigs
6. 19 mooshrooms
7. 32 potions of Strength
8. 11 times

PAGE 81

9. 5 flowers
10. 5 times
11. 84 lapis lazuli ore
12. 5 iron blocks

PAGE 82

13. 7 bottles
14. 9 trees
15. 80 mobs

Hardcore mode

5 milk, 6 sugar

PAGE 83

PVP Showdown

Alex: 91   Steve: 64

PAGE 84

1. 22 items
2. 2 mobs
3. 42 diamonds
4. 36 farm animals

PAGE 85

5. 12 zombies
6. 51 emeralds
7. 36 beacons
8. 24 rails

PAGE 86

9. 18 mobs
10. 32 enchanted items
11. 14 arrows
12. 26 creepers

PAGE 87

13. 28 potions
14. 53 animals
15. 84 Ender charges

Hardcore mode

12 items

PAGE 88

PVP Showdown

Alex: 82   Steve: 72

PAGE 89

1. 10 bow and arrows, 3 left over
2. 6 rivers, 3 lily pads left over
3. 3 rows, 3 cactuses left over
4. 8 items, 3 items left over

PAGE 90

5. 6 minutes, 2 minutes left over
6. 8 snow golems, 3 snowballs left over
7. 9 trees, 4 swings
8. 21 Eyes of Ender, 3 Ender pearls left over

PAGE 91

1. 2,160 items
2. 10 days
3. 414 hunger points
4. 31 zombie villagers

PAGE 92

5. 46 experience points.
6. 28 boats
7. 366 donkeys

Hardcore mode

Dad: 265   Mom: 245 minutes

PAGE 93

PVP Showdown

Alex: 318   Steve: 221

PAGE 94

1. $3/4$ of the Endermen
2. $1/6$ of the fireballs inflict damage
3. $3/4$ of the cobblestone structure
4. $11/16$ of the villagers

PAGE 95

5. $1/3$ of the zombies
6. $5/9$ of your weapons
7. $3/5$ of your potions
8. $1/7$ of your armor

PAGE 96

1. $7/12$ of the hostile mobs remain
2. $7/9$ of your gold ingots
3. $5/12$ of your wooden sticks
4. $1/15$ of your battles

PAGE 97

5. $19/21$ of your diamonds
6. $1/2$ of your inventory
7. $4/5$ of your fish

Hardcore mode

Answers may vary.

PAGE 98

PVP Showdown

Alex: $38/8 = 4\,3/4$ **Steve: $33/6 = 5\,1/2$**

MATH FOR MINECRAFTERS

MATH FACTS

MULTIPLICATION MATH FACTS WITH 2

1. 1
    x 2

2. 2
    x 2

3. 3
    x 2

4. 4
    x 2

5. 5
    x 2

6. 6
    x 2

7. 7
    x 2

8. 8
    x 2

9. 9
    x 2

10. 10
    x 2

11. 2
    x 1

12. 2
    x 5

13. 2
    x 3

14. 2
    x 6

15. 2
    x 8

16. 2
    x 4

17. 2
    x 0

18. 2
    x 7

19. 2
    x 10

20. 2
    x 9

MULTIPLICATION MATH FACTS WITH 2

1. 7
   x 2

2. 3
   x 2

3. 2
   x 2

4. 10
   x 2

5. 4
   x 2

6. 6
   x 2

7. 1
   x 2

8. 9
   x 2

9. 8
   x 2

10. 5
    x 2

11. 2
    x 3

12. 2
    x 7

13. 2
    x 1

14. 2
    x 10

15. 2
    x 8

16. 2
    x 4

17. 2
    x 0

18. 2
    x 5

19. 2
    x 9

20. 2
    x 6

DIVISION MATH FACTS WITH 2

1. 10
    ÷ 2

2. 2
    ÷ 2

3. 4
    ÷ 2

4. 8
    ÷ 2

5. 6
    ÷ 2

6. 2
    ÷ 1

7. 0
    ÷ 2

8. 12
    ÷ 2

9. 20
    ÷ 2

10. 40
    ÷ 2

11. 22
    ÷ 2

12. 18
    ÷ 2

13. 24
    ÷ 2

14. 80
    ÷ 2

15. 16
    ÷ 2

16. 14
    ÷ 2

17. 100
    ÷ 2

18. 60
    ÷ 2

19. 50
    ÷ 2

20. 26
    ÷ 2

DIVISION MATH FACTS WITH 2

1. 20
÷ 2

2. 0
÷ 2

3. 8
÷ 2

4. 18
÷ 2

5. 6
÷ 2

6. 22
÷ 2

7. 2
÷ 1

8. 24
÷ 2

9. 10
÷ 2

10. 14
÷ 2

11. 2
÷ 2

12. 100
÷ 2

13. 12
÷ 2

14. 50
÷ 2

15. 60
÷ 2

16. 4
÷ 2

17. 40
÷ 2

18. 16
÷ 2

19. 80
÷ 2

20. 26
÷ 2

MULTIPLICATION MATH FACTS WITH 5

1. 1
   x 5

2. 2
   x 5

3. 3
   x 5

4. 4
   x 5

5. 5
   x 5

6. 6
   x 5

7. 7
   x 5

8. 8
   x 5

9. 9
   x 5

10. 10
    x 5

11. 5
    x 1

12. 5
    x 6

13. 5
    x 3

14. 5
    x 2

15. 5
    x 8

16. 5
    x 4

17. 5
    x 0

18. 5
    x 7

19. 5
    x 10

20. 5
    x 9

MULTIPLICATION MATH FACTS WITH 5

1.   5
  x 9

2.   2
  x 5

3.   5
  x 1

4.   5
  x 6

5.   5
  x 3

6.   5
  x 7

7.   5
  x 8

8.   5
  x 4

9.   5
  x 0

10.   5
  x 2

11.   5
  x 10

12.   5
  x 5

13.   8
  x 5

14.   9
  x 5

15.   4
  x 5

16.   6
  x 5

17.   3
  x 5

18.   1
  x 5

19.   10
  x 5

20.   7
  x 5

DIVISION MATH FACTS WITH 5

1. 10
   ÷ 5

2. 30
   ÷ 5

3. 15
   ÷ 5

4. 5
   ÷ 5

5. 20
   ÷ 5

6. 5
   ÷ 1

7. 0
   ÷ 5

8. 25
   ÷ 5

9. 45
   ÷ 5

10. 30
    ÷ 5

11. 15
    ÷ 5

12. 20
    ÷ 5

13. 5
    ÷ 5

14. 40
    ÷ 5

15. 50
    ÷ 5

16. 55
    ÷ 5

17. 5
    ÷ 1

18. 35
    ÷ 5

19. 10
    ÷ 5

20. 60
    ÷ 5

DIVISION MATH FACTS WITH 5

1. 20 ÷ 5

2. 30 ÷ 5

3. 50 ÷ 5

4. 55 ÷ 5

5. 10 ÷ 5

6. 0 ÷ 5

7. 5 ÷ 1

8. 100 ÷ 5

9. 25 ÷ 5

10. 60 ÷ 5

11. 5 ÷ 5

12. 20 ÷ 5

13. 5 ÷ 1

14. 40 ÷ 5

15. 15 ÷ 5

16. 35 ÷ 5

17. 5 ÷ 5

18. 45 ÷ 5

19. 10 ÷ 5

20. 30 ÷ 5

MULTIPLICATION MATH FACTS WITH 10

1.   1
   x 10

2.   2
   x 10

3.   3
   x 10

4.   4
   x 10

5.   5
   x 10

6.   6
   x 10

7.   7
   x 10

8.   8
   x 10

9.   9
   x 10

10.   10
    x 10

11.   10
    x 1

12.   10
    x 6

13.   10
    x 3

14.   10
    x 2

15.   10
    x 8

16.   10
    x 4

17.   10
    x 0

18.   10
    x 7

19.   10
    x 10

20.   10
    x 9

MULTIPLICATION MATH FACTS WITH 10

1. 10
   x 6

2. 10
   x 1

3. 10
   x 3

4. 10
   x 2

5. 10
   x 8

6. 10
   x 0

7. 10
   x 4

8. 10
   x 7

9. 10
   x 10

10. 10
    x 9

11. 2
    x 10

12. 1
    x 10

13. 3
    x 10

14. 4
    x 10

15. 5
    x 10

16. 7
    x 10

17. 6
    x 10

18. 8
    x 10

19. 9
    x 10

20. 10
    x 10

DIVISION MATH FACTS WITH 10

1. 10
   ÷10

2. 10
   ÷ 1

3. 30
   ÷10

4. 80
   ÷10

5. 10
   ÷ 5

6. 50
   ÷10

7. 70
   ÷10

8. 40
   ÷10

9. 100
   ÷10

10. 20
    ÷10

11. 0
    ÷ 10

12. 90
    ÷10

13. 30
    ÷10

14. 60
    ÷10

15. 10
    ÷ 2

16. 80
    ÷10

17. 10
    ÷ 1

18. 50
    ÷10

19. 70
    ÷10

20. 200
    ÷10

DIVISION MATH FACTS WITH 10

1. 100
÷10

2. 10
÷ 2

3. 30
÷10

4. 80
÷10

5. 90
÷10

6. 50
÷10

7. 40
÷10

8. 70
÷10

9. 20
÷10

10. 60
÷10

11. 0
÷ 10

12. 10
÷10

13. 100
÷ 10

14. 90
÷10

15. 10
÷ 1

16. 80
÷10

17. 10
÷ 5

18. 200
÷10

19. 10
÷10

20. 50
÷10

MULTIPLICATION MATH FACTS WITH 0 AND 1

1. 7
    x 0

2. 10
    x 1

3. 2
    x 1

4. 9
    x 1

5. 7
    x 1

6. 6
    x 0

7. 3
    x 1

8. 1
    x 1

9. 4
    x 0

10. 10
    x 0

11. 8
    x 0

12. 0
    x 0

13. 2
    x 0

14. 6
    x 1

15. 8
    x 1

16. 9
    x 0

17. 1
    x 0

18. 3
    x 0

19. 5
    x 0

20. 4
    x 1

MULTIPLICATION MATH FACTS WITH 0 AND 1

1. 0
   x 0

2. 1
   x 1

3. 9
   x 1

4. 3
   x 1

5. 2
   x 1

6. 1
   x 0

7. 5
   x 1

8. 10
   x 1

9. 4
   x 0

10. 3
    x 0

11. 9
    x 0

12. 8
    x 0

13. 7
    x 1

14. 6
    x 1

15. 4
    x 1

16. 7
    x 0

17. 1
    x 10

18. 2
    x 0

19. 5
    x 0

20. 8
    x 1

DIVISION MATH FACTS WITH 0 AND 1

1. $0 \div 5$

2. $10 \div 1$

3. $0 \div 2$

4. $12 \div 1$

5. $0 \div 7$

6. $2 \div 1$

7. $0 \div 15$

8. $0 \div 4$

9. $4 \div 1$

10. $0 \div 6$

11. $1 \div 1$

12. $7 \div 1$

13. $0 \div 8$

14. $0 \div 1$

15. $0 \div 3$

16. $14 \div 1$

17. $0 \div 9$

18. $5 \div 1$

19. $20 \div 1$

20. $0 \div 10$

DIVISION MATH FACTS WITH 0 AND 1

1. 10
÷ 1

2. 0
÷ 1

3. 0
÷ 2

4. 8
÷ 1

5. 5
÷ 1

6. 2
÷ 1

7. 15
÷ 1

8. 0
÷ 3

9. 6
÷ 1

10. 0
÷ 10

11. 0
÷ 8

12. 12
÷ 1

13. 1
÷ 1

14. 0
÷ 5

15. 20
÷ 1

16. 4
÷ 1

17. 0
÷ 9

18. 0
÷ 5

19. 7
÷ 1

20. 0
÷ 4

MULTIPLICATION MATH FACTS WITH 3

1. 3
    x 2

2. 3
    x 4

3. 3
    x 10

4. 1
    x 3

5. 3
    x 3

6. 3
    x 7

7. 3
    x 9

8. 3
    x 1

9. 3
    x 8

10. 5
    x 3

11. 4
    x 3

12. 3
    x 6

13. 10
    x 3

14. 7
    x 3

15. 8
    x 3

16. 9
    x 3

17. 2
    x 3

18. 3
    x 3

19. 6
    x 3

20. 0
    x 3

MULTIPLICATION MATH FACTS WITH 3

1. 4
   x 3

2. 3
   x 6

3. 3
   x 1

4. 7
   x 3

5. 8
   x 3

6. 9
   x 3

7. 2
   x 3

8. 3
   x 3

9. 6
   x 3

10. 0
    x 3

11. 3
    x 2

12. 3
    x 4

13. 3
    x 5

14. 1
    x 3

15. 10
    x 3

16. 3
    x 7

17. 3
    x 9

18. 3
    x 1

19. 3
    x 8

20. 5
    x 3

DIVISION MATH FACTS WITH 3

1. 6 ÷ 3

2. 15 ÷ 3

3. 30 ÷ 3

4. 3 ÷ 1

5. 9 ÷ 3

6. 15 ÷ 3

7. 0 ÷ 3

8. 24 ÷ 3

9. 21 ÷ 3

10. 18 ÷ 3

11. 33 ÷ 3

12. 36 ÷ 3

13. 3 ÷ 3

14. 27 ÷ 3

15. 12 ÷ 3

16. 60 ÷ 3

17. 90 ÷ 3

18. 15 ÷ 3

19. 9 ÷ 3

20. 24 ÷ 3

DIVISION MATH FACTS WITH 3

1. 33
÷ 3

2. 15
÷ 3

3. 3
÷ 3

4. 3
÷ 1

5. 9
÷ 3

6. 18
÷ 3

7. 0
÷ 3

8. 60
÷ 3

9. 6
÷ 3

10. 99
÷ 3

11. 21
÷ 3

12. 36
÷ 3

13. 90
÷ 3

14. 24
÷ 3

15. 27
÷ 3

16. 12
÷ 3

17. 30
÷ 3

18. 0
÷ 3

19. 15
÷ 3

20. 39
÷ 3

MULTIPLICATION MATH FACTS WITH 4

1. 9
    x 4

2. 7
    x 4

3. 4
    x 4

4. 4
    x 3

5. 5
    x 4

6. 8
    x 4

7. 2
    x 4

8. 4
    x 6

9. 1
    x 4

10. 4
     x 0

11. 4
     x 2

12. 4
     x 1

13. 6
     x 4

14. 7
     x 4

15. 8
     x 4

16. 4
     x 10

17. 4
     x 9

18. 0
     x 4

19. 4
     x 8

20. 4
     x 4

MULTIPLICATION MATH FACTS WITH 4

1. 6
    × 4

2. 3
    × 4

3. 4
    × 4

4. 4
    × 2

5. 1
    × 4

6. 9
    × 4

7. 2
    × 4

8. 10
    × 4

9. 4
    × 6

10. 0
     × 4

11. 4
     × 7

12. 4
     × 9

13. 4
     × 1

14. 4
     × 8

15. 5
     × 4

16. 4
     × 4

17. 4
     × 6

18. 4
     × 3

19. 7
     × 4

20. 8
     × 4

DIVISION MATH FACTS WITH 4

1. 12 ÷ 4

2. 8 ÷ 4

3. 16 ÷ 4

4. 48 ÷ 4

5. 24 ÷ 4

6. 20 ÷ 4

7. 4 ÷ 4

8. 40 ÷ 4

9. 4 ÷ 1

10. 44 ÷ 4

11. 80 ÷ 4

12. 36 ÷ 4

13. 28 ÷ 4

14. 0 ÷ 4

15. 24 ÷ 4

16. 32 ÷ 4

17. 4 ÷ 4

18. 12 ÷ 4

19. 16 ÷ 4

20. 60 ÷ 4

DIVISION MATH FACTS WITH 4

1. 28 ÷ 4

2. 16 ÷ 4

3. 8 ÷ 4

4. 40 ÷ 4

5. 24 ÷ 4

6. 32 ÷ 4

7. 0 ÷ 4

8. 4 ÷ 4

9. 4 ÷ 1

10. 44 ÷ 4

11. 80 ÷ 4

12. 32 ÷ 4

13. 12 ÷ 4

14. 0 ÷ 4

15. 20 ÷ 4

16. 36 ÷ 4

17. 44 ÷ 4

18. 16 ÷ 4

19. 8 ÷ 4

20. 4 ÷ 4

MULTIPLICATION MATH FACTS WITH 6

1. $\begin{array}{r} 6 \\ \times\ 2 \\ \hline \end{array}$

2. $\begin{array}{r} 6 \\ \times\ 4 \\ \hline \end{array}$

3. $\begin{array}{r} 6 \\ \times\ 6 \\ \hline \end{array}$

4. $\begin{array}{r} 12 \\ \times\ 6 \\ \hline \end{array}$

5. $\begin{array}{r} 10 \\ \times\ 6 \\ \hline \end{array}$

6. $\begin{array}{r} 6 \\ \times\ 7 \\ \hline \end{array}$

7. $\begin{array}{r} 6 \\ \times\ 9 \\ \hline \end{array}$

8. $\begin{array}{r} 6 \\ \times\ 1 \\ \hline \end{array}$

9. $\begin{array}{r} 6 \\ \times\ 8 \\ \hline \end{array}$

10. $\begin{array}{r} 5 \\ \times\ 6 \\ \hline \end{array}$

11. $\begin{array}{r} 6 \\ \times\ 6 \\ \hline \end{array}$

12. $\begin{array}{r} 3 \\ \times\ 6 \\ \hline \end{array}$

13. $\begin{array}{r} 6 \\ \times\ 0 \\ \hline \end{array}$

14. $\begin{array}{r} 7 \\ \times\ 6 \\ \hline \end{array}$

15. $\begin{array}{r} 8 \\ \times\ 6 \\ \hline \end{array}$

16. $\begin{array}{r} 9 \\ \times\ 6 \\ \hline \end{array}$

17. $\begin{array}{r} 2 \\ \times\ 6 \\ \hline \end{array}$

18. $\begin{array}{r} 6 \\ \times\ 3 \\ \hline \end{array}$

19. $\begin{array}{r} 6 \\ \times\ 11 \\ \hline \end{array}$

20. $\begin{array}{r} 0 \\ \times\ 6 \\ \hline \end{array}$

MULTIPLICATION MATH FACTS WITH 6

1. $\begin{array}{r} 6 \\ \times\ 6 \\ \hline \end{array}$

2. $\begin{array}{r} 3 \\ \times\ 6 \\ \hline \end{array}$

3. $\begin{array}{r} 6 \\ \times\ 1 \\ \hline \end{array}$

4. $\begin{array}{r} 7 \\ \times\ 6 \\ \hline \end{array}$

5. $\begin{array}{r} 8 \\ \times\ 6 \\ \hline \end{array}$

6. $\begin{array}{r} 4 \\ \times\ 6 \\ \hline \end{array}$

7. $\begin{array}{r} 2 \\ \times\ 6 \\ \hline \end{array}$

8. $\begin{array}{r} 6 \\ \times\ 3 \\ \hline \end{array}$

9. $\begin{array}{r} 6 \\ \times\ 12 \\ \hline \end{array}$

10. $\begin{array}{r} 0 \\ \times\ 6 \\ \hline \end{array}$

11. $\begin{array}{r} 6 \\ \times\ 2 \\ \hline \end{array}$

12. $\begin{array}{r} 6 \\ \times\ 5 \\ \hline \end{array}$

13. $\begin{array}{r} 6 \\ \times\ 11 \\ \hline \end{array}$

14. $\begin{array}{r} 12 \\ \times\ 6 \\ \hline \end{array}$

15. $\begin{array}{r} 10 \\ \times\ 6 \\ \hline \end{array}$

16. $\begin{array}{r} 6 \\ \times\ 9 \\ \hline \end{array}$

17. $\begin{array}{r} 6 \\ \times\ 7 \\ \hline \end{array}$

18. $\begin{array}{r} 6 \\ \times\ 10 \\ \hline \end{array}$

19. $\begin{array}{r} 8 \\ \times\ 6 \\ \hline \end{array}$

20. $\begin{array}{r} 5 \\ \times\ 6 \\ \hline \end{array}$

DIVISION MATH FACTS WITH 6

1. $36 \div 6$

2. $42 \div 6$

3. $60 \div 6$

4. $6 \div 1$

5. $12 \div 6$

6. $18 \div 6$

7. $6 \div 6$

8. $54 \div 6$

9. $24 \div 6$

10. $72 \div 6$

11. $66 \div 6$

12. $30 \div 6$

13. $0 \div 6$

14. $48 \div 6$

15. $18 \div 6$

16. $60 \div 6$

17. $6 \div 1$

18. $42 \div 6$

19. $36 \div 6$

20. $54 \div 6$

DIVISION MATH FACTS WITH 6

1. 66 ÷ 6

2. 30 ÷ 6

3. 0 ÷ 6

4. 48 ÷ 6

5. 18 ÷ 6

6. 60 ÷ 6

7. 6 ÷ 1

8. 42 ÷ 6

9. 36 ÷ 6

10. 54 ÷ 6

11. 6 ÷ 2

12. 42 ÷ 6

13. 60 ÷ 6

14. 6 ÷ 3

15. 12 ÷ 6

16. 18 ÷ 6

17. 6 ÷ 6

18. 54 ÷ 6

19. 24 ÷ 6

20. 72 ÷ 6

MULTIPLICATION MATH FACTS WITH 7

1. 6
   x 7

2. 3
   x 7

3. 7
   x 1

4. 7
   x 5

5. 8
   x 7

6. 4
   x 7

7. 2
   x 7

8. 7
   x 3

9. 7
   x 12

10. 0
   x 7

11. 7
   x 2

12. 5
   x 7

13. 7
   x 11

14. 12
   x 7

15. 10
   x 7

16. 7
   x 9

17. 7
   x 7

18. 7
   x 10

19. 7
   x 8

20. 11
   x 7

MULTIPLICATION MATH FACTS WITH 7

1. 7
    x 2

2. 7
    x 4

3. 7
    x 7

4. 12
    x 7

5. 10
    x 7

6. 7
    x 3

7. 7
    x 9

8. 7
    x 1

9. 7
    x 8

10. 5
     x 7

11. 4
     x 7

12. 3
     x 7

13. 7
     x 10

14. 7
     x 5

15. 8
     x 7

16. 9
     x 7

17. 2
     x 7

18. 7
     x 3

19. 7
     x 11

20. 0
     x 7

DIVISION MATH FACTS WITH 7

1. 49 ÷ 7

2. 42 ÷ 7

3. 14 ÷ 7

4. 28 ÷ 7

5. 35 ÷ 7

6. 70 ÷ 7

7. 56 ÷ 7

8. 7 ÷ 1

9. 63 ÷ 7

10. 77 ÷ 7

11. 7 ÷ 7

12. 21 ÷ 7

13. 0 ÷ 7

14. 49 ÷ 7

15. 84 ÷ 7

16. 14 ÷ 7

17. 42 ÷ 7

18. 35 ÷ 7

19. 7 ÷ 1

20. 70 ÷ 7

DIVISION MATH FACTS WITH 7

1. 42
÷ 7

2. 63
÷ 7

3. 70
÷ 7

4. 49
÷ 7

5. 77
÷ 7

6. 14
÷ 7

7. 56
÷ 7

8. 7
÷ 1

9. 28
÷ 7

10. 35
÷ 7

11. 77
÷ 7

12. 21
÷ 7

13. 7
÷ 7

14. 70
÷ 7

15. 42
÷ 7

16. 0
÷ 7

17. 84
÷ 7

18. 49
÷ 7

19. 7
÷ 1

20. 70
÷ 7

MULTIPLICATION MATH FACTS WITH 8

1. 8
    x 2

2. 8
    x 4

3. 8
    x 8

4. 12
    x 8

5. 10
    x 8

6. 8
    x 3

7. 8
    x 9

8. 8
    x 1

9. 8
    x 0

10. 5
     x 8

11. 4
     x 8

12. 3
     x 8

13. 8
     x 10

14. 8
     x 5

15. 8
     x 8

16. 9
     x 8

17. 2
     x 8

18. 8
     x 3

19. 8
     x 11

20. 0
     x 8

MULTIPLICATION MATH FACTS WITH 8

1. 6
   x 8

2. 3
   x 8

3. 8
   x 1

4. 8
   x 11

5. 8
   x 8

6. 4
   x 8

7. 2
   x 8

8. 8
   x 3

9. 8
   x 12

10. 0
    x 8

11. 8
    x 2

12. 5
    x 8

13. 8
    x 11

14. 12
    x 8

15. 10
    x 8

16. 8
    x 9

17. 8
    x 8

18. 8
    x 10

19. 8
    x 1

20. 5
    x 8

DIVISION MATH FACTS WITH 8

1. 16
    ÷ 8

2. 64
    ÷ 8

3. 32
    ÷ 8

4. 8
    ÷ 1

5. 56
    ÷ 8

6. 72
    ÷ 8

7. 8
    ÷ 8

8. 24
    ÷ 8

9. 40
    ÷ 8

10. 48
     ÷ 8

11. 88
     ÷ 8

12. 80
     ÷ 8

13. 0
     ÷ 8

14. 32
     ÷ 8

15. 96
     ÷ 8

16. 8
     ÷ 4

17. 16
     ÷ 8

18. 56
     ÷ 8

19. 8
     ÷ 2

20. 0
     ÷ 8

DIVISION MATH FACTS WITH 8

1. $88 \div 8$

2. $80 \div 8$

3. $0 \div 8$

4. $32 \div 8$

5. $8 \div 8$

6. $8 \div 2$

7. $16 \div 8$

8. $56 \div 8$

9. $8 \div 4$

10. $0 \div 8$

11. $24 \div 8$

12. $96 \div 8$

13. $64 \div 8$

14. $40 \div 8$

15. $48 \div 8$

16. $8 \div 8$

17. $64 \div 8$

18. $32 \div 8$

19. $8 \div 1$

20. $56 \div 8$

MULTIPLICATION MATH FACTS WITH 9

1.   6
  x 9

2.   3
  x 9

3.   9
  x 1

4.   9
  x 11

5.   9
  x 9

6.   4
  x 9

7.   2
  x 9

8.   9
  x 3

9.   9
  x 12

10.   0
  x 9

11.   9
  x 2

12.   5
  x 9

13.   9
  x 11

14. 12
  x 9

15. 10
  x 9

16.   9
  x 9

17.   1
  x 9

18.   9
  x 10

19.   9
  x 4

20.   5
  x 9

MULTIPLICATION MATH FACTS WITH 9

1. 9
   x 2

2. 9
   x 4

3. 9
   x 9

4. 12
   x 9

5. 10
   x 9

6. 9
   x 3

7. 8
   x 9

8. 9
   x 1

9. 9
   x 0

10. 5
    x 9

11. 4
    x 9

12. 3
    x 9

13. 9
    x 10

14. 9
    x 5

15. 9
    x 9

16. 9
    x 8

17. 2
    x 9

18. 9
    x 3

19. 9
    x 11

20. 0
    x 9

DIVISION MATH FACTS WITH 9

1. 90
    ÷ 9

2. 27
    ÷ 9

3. 81
    ÷ 9

4. 99
    ÷ 9

5. 72
    ÷ 9

6. 9
    ÷ 9

7. 36
    ÷ 9

8. 54
    ÷ 9

9. 45
    ÷ 9

10. 9
     ÷ 1

11. 0
     ÷ 9

12. 18
     ÷ 9

13. 108
     ÷ 9

14. 63
     ÷ 9

15. 27
     ÷ 9

16. 72
     ÷ 9

17. 54
     ÷ 9

18. 0
     ÷ 9

19. 9
     ÷ 1

20. 45
     ÷ 9

DIVISION MATH FACTS WITH 9

1. $99 \div 9$

2. $18 \div 9$

3. $108 \div 9$

4. $63 \div 9$

5. $27 \div 9$

6. $81 \div 9$

7. $54 \div 9$

8. $0 \div 9$

9. $9 \div 1$

10. $45 \div 9$

11. $9 \div 9$

12. $27 \div 9$

13. $72 \div 9$

14. $0 \div 9$

15. $90 \div 9$

16. $18 \div 9$

17. $36 \div 9$

18. $54 \div 9$

19. $45 \div 9$

20. $9 \div 3$

ANSWERS

PAGE 104

1. 2
2. 4
3. 6
4. 8
5. 10
6. 12
7. 14
8. 16
9. 18
10. 20
11. 2
12. 10
13. 6
14. 12
15. 16
16. 8
17. 0
18. 14
19. 20
20. 18

PAGE 105

1. 14
2. 6
3. 4
4. 20
5. 8
6. 12
7. 2
8. 18
9. 16
10. 10
11. 6
12. 14
13. 2
14. 20
15. 16
16. 8
17. 0
18. 10
19. 18
20. 12

PAGE 106

1. 5
2. 1
3. 2
4. 4
5. 3
6. 2
7. 0
8. 6
9. 10
10. 20
11. 11
12. 9
13. 12
14. 40
15. 8
16. 7
17. 50
18. 30
19. 25
20. 13

PAGE 107

1. 10
2. 0
3. 4
4. 9
5. 3
6. 11
7. 2
8. 12
9. 5
10. 7
11. 1
12. 50
13. 6
14. 25
15. 30
16. 2
17. 20
18. 8
19. 40
20. 13

PAGE 108

1. 5
2. 10
3. 15
4. 20
5. 25
6. 30
7. 35
8. 40
9. 45
10. 50
11. 5
12. 30
13. 15
14. 10
15. 40
16. 20
17. 0
18. 35
19. 50
20. 45

PAGE 109

1. 45
2. 10
3. 5
4. 30
5. 15
6. 35
7. 40
8. 20
9. 0
10. 10
11. 50
12. 25
13. 40
14. 45
15. 20
16. 30
17. 15
18. 5
19. 50
20. 35

PAGE 110

1. 2
2. 6
3. 3
4. 1
5. 4
6. 5
7. 0
8. 5
9. 9
10. 6
11. 3
12. 4
13. 1
14. 8
15. 10
16. 11
17. 5
18. 7
19. 2
20. 12

PAGE 111

1. 4
2. 6
3. 10
4. 11
5. 2
6. 0
7. 5
8. 20
9. 5
10. 12
11. 1
12. 4
13. 5
14. 8
15. 3
16. 7
17. 1
18. 9
19. 2
20. 6

PAGE 112

1. 10
2. 20
3. 30
4. 40
5. 50
6. 60
7. 70
8. 80
9. 90
10. 100
11. 10
12. 60
13. 30
14. 20
15. 80
16. 40
17. 0
18. 70
19. 100
20. 90

PAGE 113

1. 60
2. 10
3. 30
4. 20
5. 80
6. 0
7. 40
8. 70
9. 100
10. 90
11. 20
12. 10
13. 30
14. 40
15. 50
16. 70
17. 60
18. 80
19. 90
20. 100

PAGE 114

1. 1
2. 10
3. 3
4. 8
5. 2
6. 5
7. 7
8. 4
9. 10
10. 2
11. 0
12. 9
13. 3
14. 6
15. 5
16. 8
17. 10
18. 5
19. 7
20. 20

PAGE 115

1. 10
2. 5
3. 3
4. 8
5. 9
6. 5
7. 4
8. 7
9. 2
10. 6
11. 0
12. 1
13. 10
14. 9
15. 10
16. 8
17. 2
18. 20
19. 1
20. 5

PAGE 116

1. 0
2. 10
3. 2
4. 9
5. 7
6. 0
7. 3
8. 1
9. 0
10. 0
11. 0
12. 0
13. 0
14. 6
15. 8
16. 0
17. 0
18. 0
19. 0
20. 4

PAGE 117

1. 0
2. 1
3. 9
4. 3
5. 2
6. 0
7. 5
8. 10
9. 0
10. 0
11. 0
12. 0
13. 7
14. 6
15. 4
16. 0
17. 10
18. 0
19. 0
20. 8

PAGE 118

1. 0
2. 10
3. 0
4. 12
5. 0
6. 2
7. 0
8. 0
9. 4
10. 0
11. 1
12. 7
13. 0
14. 0
15. 0
16. 14
17. 0
18. 5
19. 20
20. 0

PAGE 119

1. 10
2. 0
3. 0
4. 8
5. 5
6. 2
7. 15
8. 0
9. 6
10. 0
11. 0
12. 12
13. 1
14. 0
15. 20
16. 4
17. 0
18. 0
19. 7
20. 0

PAGE 120

1. 6
2. 12
3. 30
4. 3
5. 9
6. 21
7. 27
8. 3
9. 24
10. 15
11. 12
12. 18
13. 30
14. 21
15. 24
16. 27
17. 6
18. 9
19. 18
20. 0

PAGE 121

1. 12
2. 18
3. 3
4. 21
5. 24
6. 27
7. 6
8. 9
9. 18
10. 0
11. 6
12. 12
13. 15
14. 3
15. 30
16. 21
17. 27
18. 3
19. 24
20. 15

PAGE 122

1. 2
2. 5
3. 10
4. 3
5. 3
6. 5
7. 0
8. 8
9. 7
10. 6
11. 11
12. 12
13. 1
14. 9
15. 4
16. 20
17. 30
18. 5
19. 3
20. 8

PAGE 123

1. 11
2. 5
3. 1
4. 3
5. 3
6. 6
7. 0
8. 20
9. 2
10. 33
11. 7
12. 12
13. 30
14. 8
15. 9
16. 4
17. 10
18. 0
19. 5
20. 13

PAGE 124

1. 36
2. 28
3. 16
4. 12
5. 20
6. 32
7. 8
8. 24
9. 4
10. 0
11. 8
12. 4
13. 24
14. 28
15. 32
16. 40
17. 36
18. 0
19. 32
20. 16

PAGE 125

1. 24
2. 12
3. 16
4. 8
5. 4
6. 36
7. 8
8. 40
9. 24
10. 0
11. 28
12. 36
13. 4
14. 32
15. 20
16. 16
17. 24
18. 12
19. 28
20. 32

PAGE 126

1. 3
2. 2
3. 4
4. 12
5. 6
6. 5
7. 1
8. 10
9. 4
10. 11
11. 20
12. 9
13. 7
14. 0
15. 6
16. 8
17. 1
18. 3
19. 4
20. 15

PAGE 127

1. 7
2. 4
3. 2
4. 10
5. 6
6. 8
7. 0
8. 1
9. 4
10. 11
11. 20
12. 8
13. 3
14. 0
15. 5
16. 9
17. 11
18. 4
19. 2
20. 1

PAGE 128

1. 12
2. 24
3. 36
4. 72
5. 60
6. 42
7. 54
8. 6
9. 48
10. 30
11. 36
12. 18
13. 0
14. 42
15. 48
16. 54
17. 12
18. 18
19. 66
20. 0

PAGE 129

1. 36
2. 18
3. 6
4. 42
5. 48
6. 24
7. 12
8. 18
9. 72
10. 0
11. 12
12. 30
13. 66
14. 72
15. 60
16. 54
17. 42
18. 60
19. 48
20. 30

PAGE 130

1. 6
2. 7
3. 10
4. 6
5. 2
6. 3
7. 1
8. 9
9. 4
10. 12
11. 11
12. 5
13. 0
14. 8
15. 3
16. 10
17. 6
18. 7
19. 6
20. 9

PAGE 131

1. 11
2. 5
3. 0
4. 8
5. 3
6. 10
7. 6
8. 7
9. 6
10. 9
11. 3
12. 7
13. 10
14. 2
15. 2
16. 3
17. 1
18. 9
19. 4
20. 12

147

PAGE 132

1. 42
2. 21
3. 7
4. 35
5. 56
6. 28
7. 14
8. 21
9. 84
10. 0
11. 14
12. 35
13. 77
14. 84
15. 70
16. 63
17. 49
18. 70
19. 56
20. 77

PAGE 133

1. 14
2. 28
3. 49
4. 84
5. 70
6. 21
7. 63
8. 7
9. 56
10. 35
11. 28
12. 21
13. 70
14. 35
15. 56
16. 63
17. 14
18. 21
19. 77
20. 0

PAGE 134

1. 7
2. 6
3. 2
4. 4
5. 5
6. 10
7. 8
8. 7
9. 9
10. 11
11. 1
12. 3
13. 0
14. 7
15. 12
16. 2
17. 6
18. 5
19. 7
20. 10

PAGE 135

1. 6
2. 9
3. 10
4. 7
5. 11
6. 2
7. 8
8. 7
9. 4
10. 5
11. 11
12. 3
13. 0
14. 10
15. 6
16. 0
17. 12
18. 7
19. 7
20. 10

PAGE 136

1. 16
2. 32
3. 64
4. 96
5. 80
6. 24
7. 72
8. 8
9. 0
10. 40
11. 32
12. 24
13. 80
14. 40
15. 64
16. 72
17. 16
18. 24
19. 88
20. 0

PAGE 137

1. 48
2. 24
3. 8
4. 88
5. 64
6. 32
7. 16
8. 24
9. 96
10. 0
11. 16
12. 40
13. 88
14. 96
15. 80
16. 72
17. 64
18. 80
19. 8
20. 40

PAGE 138

1. 2
2. 8
3. 4
4. 8
5. 7
6. 9
7. 1
8. 3
9. 5
10. 6
11. 11
12. 10
13. 0
14. 4
15. 12
16. 2
17. 2
18. 7
19. 4
20. 0

PAGE 139

1. 11
2. 10
3. 0
4. 4
5. 1
6. 4
7. 2
8. 7
9. 2
10. 0
11. 3
12. 12
13. 8
14. 5
15. 6
16. 1
17. 8
18. 4
19. 8
20. 7

PAGE 140

1. 54
2. 27
3. 9
4. 99
5. 81
6. 36
7. 18
8. 27
9. 108
10. 0
11. 18
12. 45
13. 99
14. 108
15. 90
16. 81
17. 9
18. 90
19. 36
20. 45

PAGE 141

1. 18
2. 36
3. 81
4. 108
5. 90
6. 27
7. 72
8. 9
9. 0
10. 45
11. 36
12. 27
13. 90
14. 45
15. 81
16. 72
17. 18
18. 27
19. 99
20. 0

PAGE 142

1. 10
2. 3
3. 9
4. 11
5. 8
6. 1
7. 4
8. 6
9. 5
10. 9
11. 0
12. 2
13. 12
14. 7
15. 3
16. 8
17. 6
18. 0
19. 9
20. 5

PAGE 143

1. 11
2. 2
3. 12
4. 7
5. 3
6. 9
7. 6
8. 0
9. 9
10. 5
11. 1
12. 3
13. 8
14. 0
15. 10
16. 2
17. 4
18. 6
19. 5
20. 3

GAMES AND PUZZLES FOR
MINECRAFTERS

AMAZING ACTIVITIES

ON THE PLAYGROUND

Take a good look to find the ten differences between these two pictures.

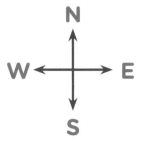

ENCHANTED MAP

This End City map is enchanted. To reveal its contents, you must press all twelve buttons in the right order and land on the F button last. Use the letters and numbers on the buttons to direct you.

Which button must you push first to get to F last?

Hint: 1N means press the button one space north; 2E means move two spaces east. W=west and S=south.

COMMON CODE

Use the key to identify three items that are familiar to Minecrafters. Then use the key to fill in the last set of blank spaces to reveal where all three items are found.

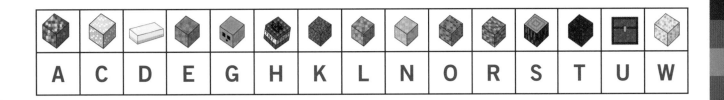

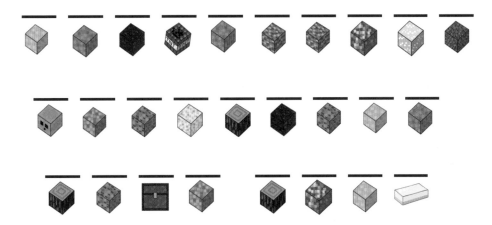

What do the three words above have in common?

They're all found in

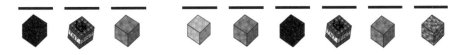

EVERY NOOK AND CRANNY

Draw a line from Start to Stop that passes through every apple once and only once. Your line can go up, down, left, or right, but not diagonally. On your mark, get set, go!

Start

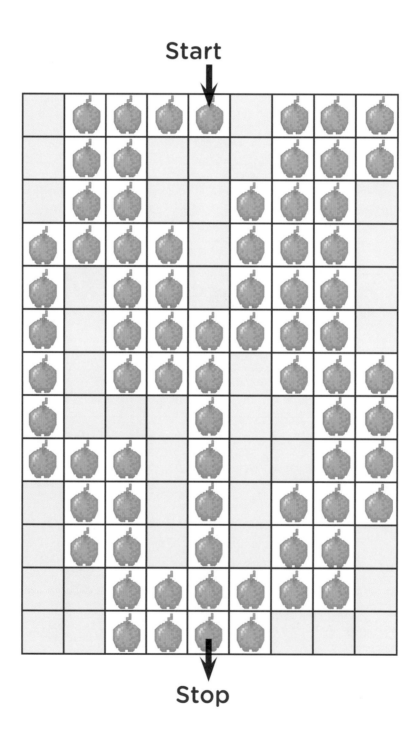

Stop

CIRCLE OF TRUTH: SURVIVAL TIP

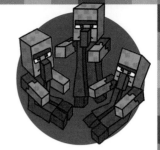

Start at the ▼. Write every third letter on the spaces to reveal a truth about Minecraft.

W_ _ _ _   _   _ _ _ _ _ _ _   _ _   _ _ _ _   _ _ _ _,

_ _ _ _   _ _ _ _ _ _ _ _   _ _ _ _   _ _ _   _ _ _ _ _   _ _ _ _   _ _ _

SKELETON TWINS

Only two of these skeletons are exactly the same. Which two are identical?
Circle the twins.

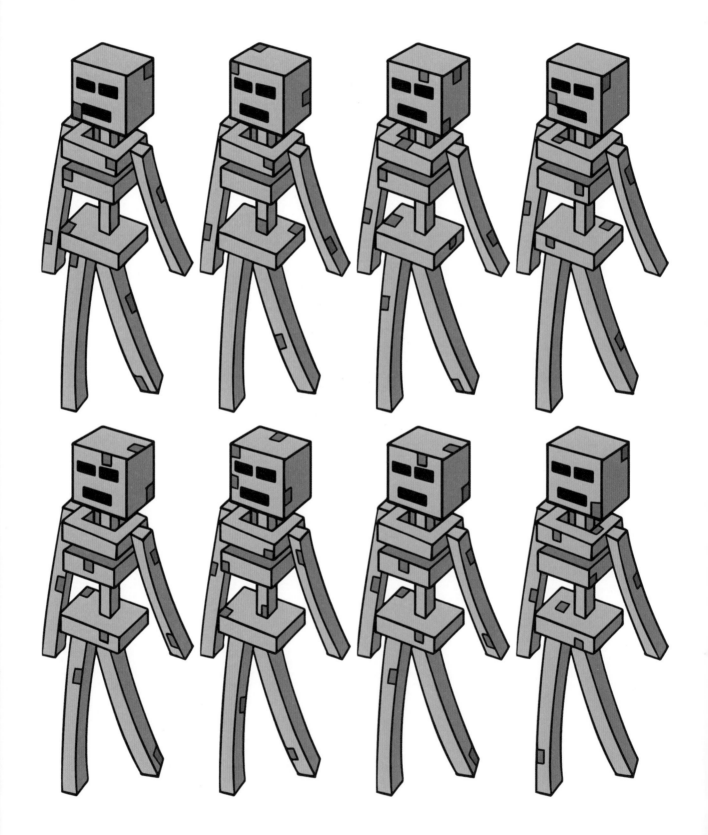

CONNECT THE DOTS: PIT OF PERIL!

Connect the dots to complete this perilous scene.

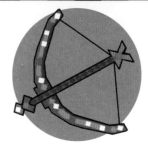

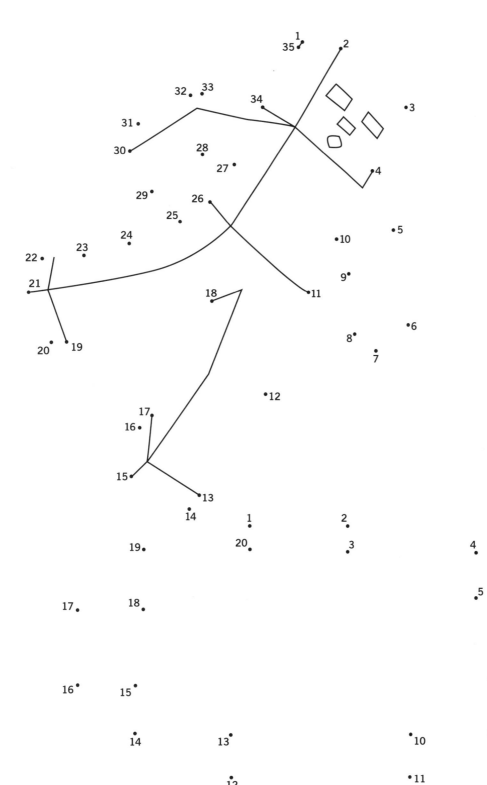

SQUARED UP: BLOCK PARTY

Each of the six blocks in this puzzle can appear only once in each row, each column, and pink rectangle. Use the letter C to represent a clay block, the letter D for a dirt block, and so on. Can you fill every square with the right letter?

 C = Clay   D = Dirt   G = Gravel   I = Ice   O = Obsidian   S = Sand

	I	G	C	O	
O	C			G	I
I		S	D		G
D		C	O		S
C	S			D	O
	D	O	I	S	

HOLD IT!

It's time to discuss a weighty matter. Start with the corner letter, then read every third letter, moving clockwise around the square, and write them in the blank spaces below until you solve the mystery message.

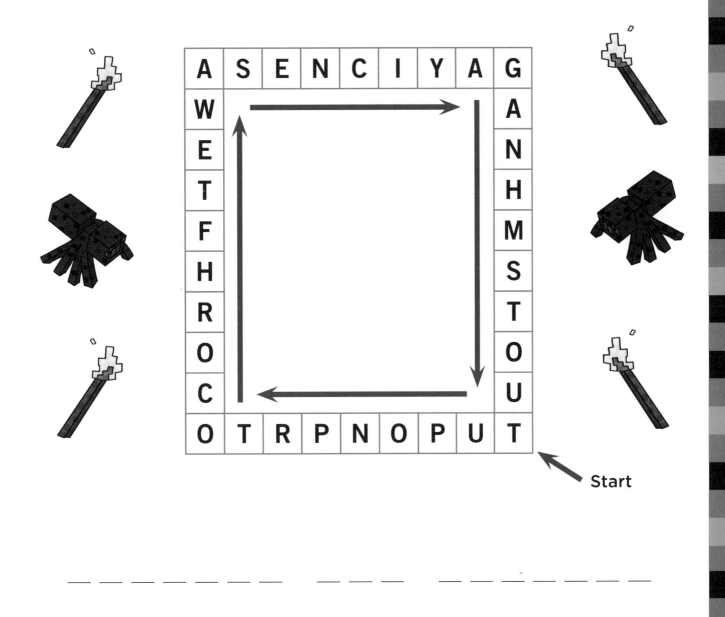

Start

_ _ _ _ _ _ _ _   _ _ _   _ _ _ _ _

_ _ _   _ _ _ _ _ _

_ _ _ _ _ _

COLLECTING TREASURE

Four treasures are yours for the taking—and you want them all! Find the path that allows you to collect the four treasures between Start and Finish. Heads up! Paths go under and over each other.

Start

Finish

CIRCLE OF TRUTH: FOOD FOR THOUGHT

Start at the ▼ .

Write every third letter on the spaces to reveal a Minecrafting secret.

▼

(Circle of letters: ...SIIENSAGHEHCAUATNUIGSNEEGRSPAPUNOFDIFSEAORUNF...)

E _ _ _ _ _   _ _ _ _ _ _ _ _ _

_ _ _ _ _ _   _ _ _ _ _ _ _ ,

_ _ _ _ _ _ , _ _ _   _ _ _ _ _ _ _

YOU CAN DRAW IT: IRON GOLEM

Use the grid to copy the picture. Examine the lines in each small square in the grid at the left, then transfer those lines to the corresponding square in the grid on the right.

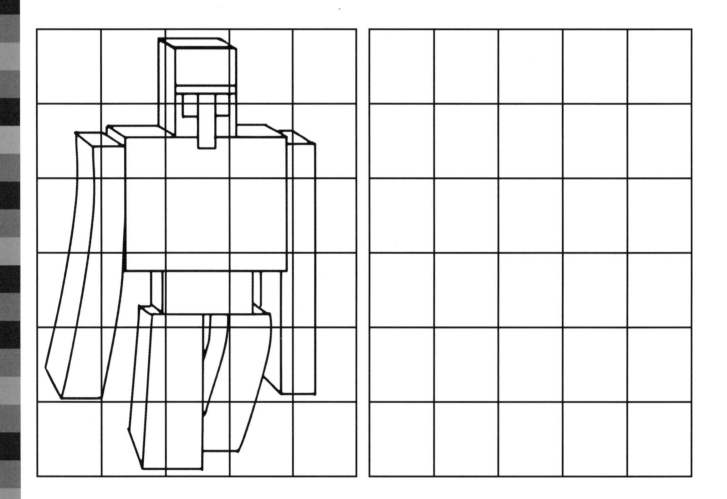

TIP FOR ENDING ENDERMEN

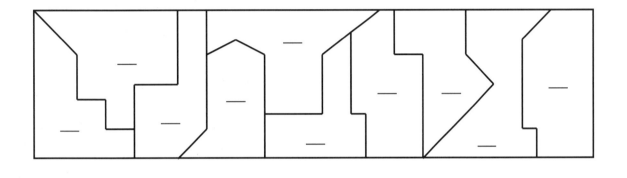

Step 1: Find the ten puzzle pieces that fit the shapes in the rectangle. Watch out! Pieces might be rotated or flipped. Write the letters of the correct pieces on the spaces. Not all pieces are used below.

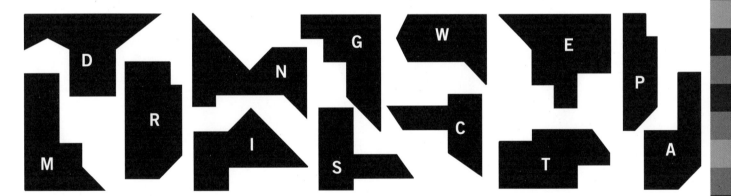

Step 2: Write the letters from the spaces above in the boxes that have the same numbers to reveal something that can help you destroy Endermen.

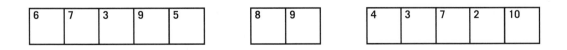

WORD FARM

The words bat, cow, pig, sheep, spider, squid, chicken, donkey, mule, polar bear, ocelot, *and* wolf *are hiding on this farm. How many words can you spot?*

CONNECT THE DOTS: FARM LIFE

Connect the dots to to see what's happening on the Minecrafter's farm.

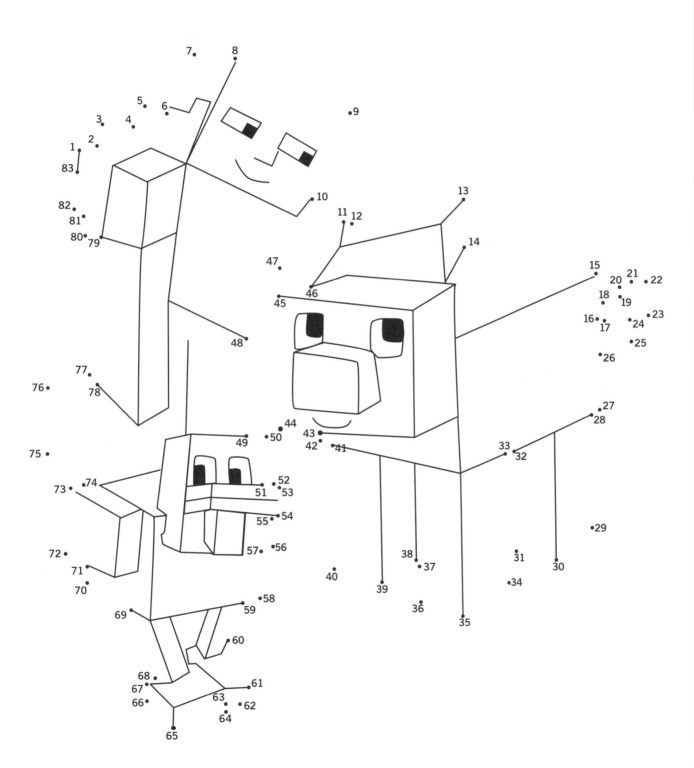

HUNT FOR ENCHANTMENTS

Find and circle the names of fifteen enchantments in the wordfind below. They might be forward, backward, up, down, or diagonal. Write unused letters on the blank spaces, in order from top to bottom and left to right, to discover a fun fact about enchantments.

Hint: *Circle individual letters instead of whole words. We've found one to get you started.*

H	O	O	K	C	A	B	K	C	O	N	K
E	F	F	I	C	I	E	N	C	Y	K	M
P	O	I	S	M	I	T	E	R	S	I	G
R	E	F	R	I	S	N	H	H	W	N	N
O	E	G	I	E	U	T	A	H	I	F	I
T	M	T	N	T	A	R	H	K	E	I	D
E	A	P	R	I	P	S	A	L	P	N	N
C	L	O	O	N	T	E	P	U	U	I	E
T	F	R	E	W	R	O	E	E	N	T	M
I	E	S	N	B	E	C	O	H	C	Y	A
O	S	N	N	T	M	R	E	L	H	T	N
N	T	U	S	I	L	K	T	O	U	C	H

EFFICIENCY
FIRE ASPECT
FLAME
FORTUNE
INFINITY
KNOCKBACK
~~LOOTING~~
MENDING
POWER
PROTECTION
PUNCH
SHARPNESS
SILK TOUCH
SMITE
UNBREAKING

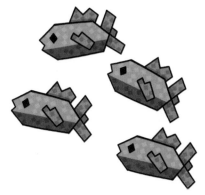

___ ___ ___ ___   ___ ___ ___ ___   ___ ___ ___   ___ ___ ___

___ ___ ___   ___ ___ ___ ___   ___ ___ ___ ___ ___ ___

ROTTEN LUCK

Take your chances with this dangerous maze and avoid food poisoning at all costs. Choose a path from the Start box. There's only one lucky path that leads to a quiet corner and a delicious cookie. The rest lead to the dreaded rotten flesh! Good luck!

Start

YOU WIN!

BAD LUCK AHEAD!

TURN BACK!

D A N G E R

MULTIPLAYER MISMATCH

These two pictures are nearly identical, except for ten little differences.
How many of these differences can you find?

TWIN MOBS

Only two of these villagers are exactly the same.
Which two are identical?

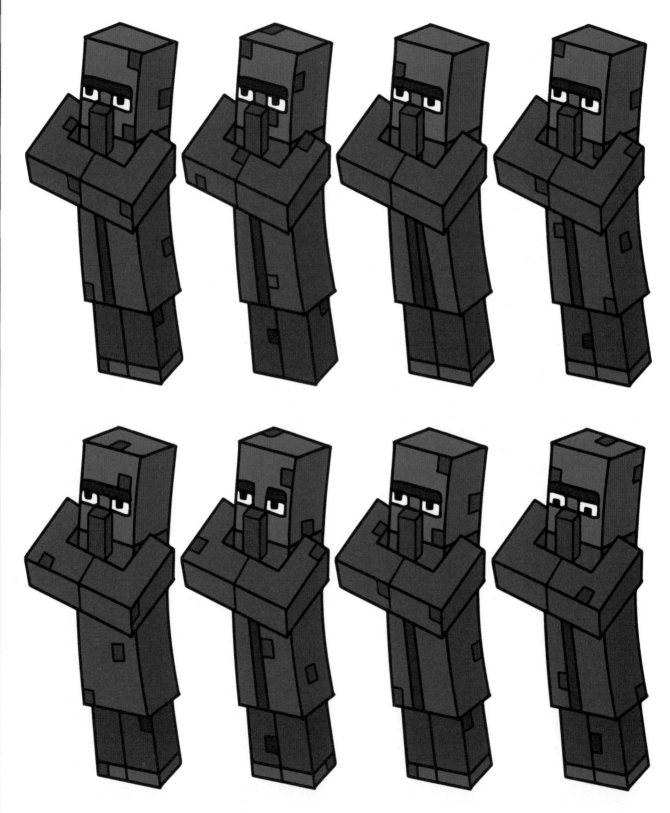

PATH OF DOOM

Begin at the dot below each player's name and work your way down to figure out how each player met their doom. Every time you hit a horizontal line (one that goes across), you must follow it.

Which player was destroyed by an exploding creeper?

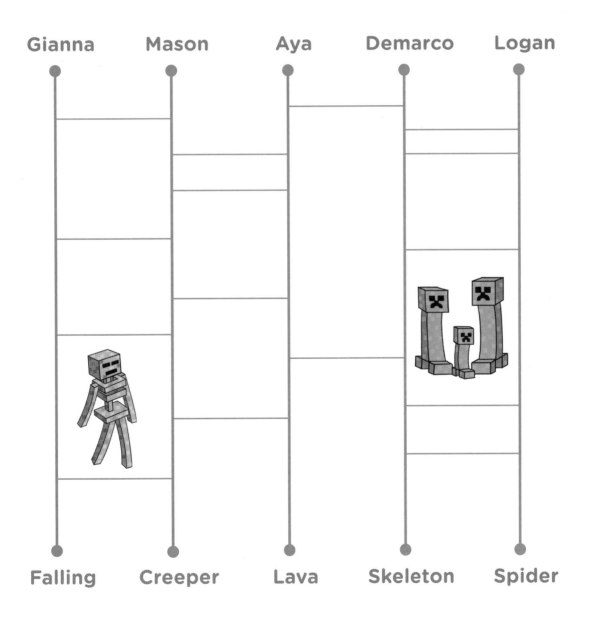

Gianna	Mason	Aya	Demarco	Logan

Falling	Creeper	Lava	Skeleton	Spider

TRUTH OR TALE?

This is a two-part puzzle. First, name the icons and figure out where each word goes in the crossword. Use the arrows to help you place the first two words. Second, transfer the numbered letters from the crossword to the numbered spaces at the bottom to reveal a claim about Minecraft.

CONNECT THE DOTS: OUR HERO

Connect the dots and find out who always saves the day.

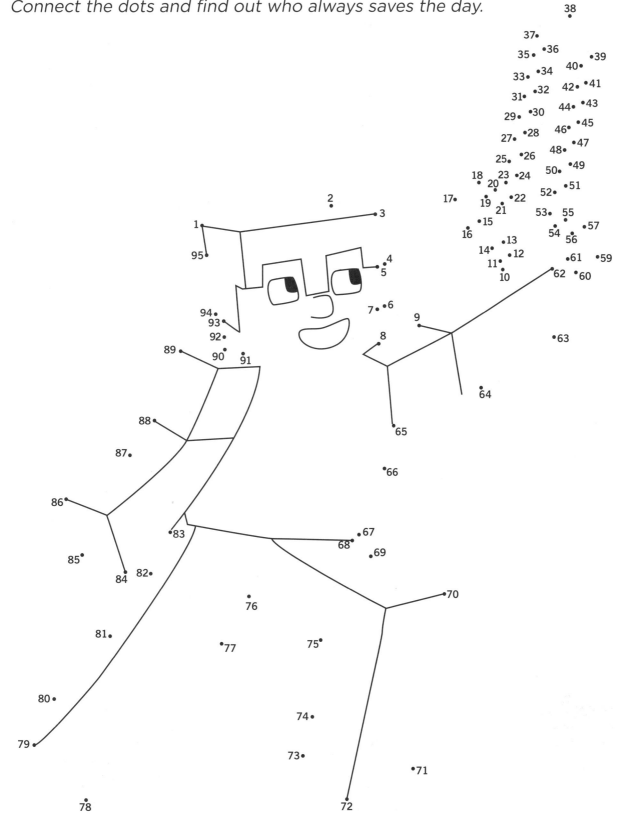

TERMS OF THE GAME

Use the clues (not the pictures this time) to find words that fit in the boxes below.

ACROSS

3   Come to life in the game world

5   An object that is fired at

8   The hunger bar is visible in this mode

9   Begin fighting with

12 Brew potions or power lights with this

15 A **COURSEER** pack allows players to customize textures, sounds, and more *(Unscramble the word on the space)*

16 This plus cocoa beans makes a cookie

17 Default game character

18 Forest or desert, for example

DOWN

1   Leafless desert plant, often with sharp spikes

2   Entryway to another world

4   Use this to make paper

6   Biome with sand dunes, dead bushes, and cacti

7   Where skin and tools are displayed

10 This type of mob runs away when hurt

11 Builder's favorite mode

13 Have lava flow on top of water to create this

14 Lava sources and random fires are hazards here

SQUARED UP: INVENTORY

Each of the six inventory items in this puzzle can appear only once in each row, each column, and pink rectangle. Use the letter A to represent apple, the letter C for carrot, and so on. Can you fill every block with the proper item?

A = Apple   **C = Carrot**   **M = Milk**   **P = Potion**   **S = Sword**   **W = Wheat**

W	S	P	C	M	
M		A			P
P				C	
C	M		A	P	S
S			P		M
	P	M		W	

FACT-FINDING MISSION

Your mission is find the fact in the letters below. Start with a letter in one of the corners (you have to figure out which one), then read every third letter, going clockwise around the square, until all of the letters are used.

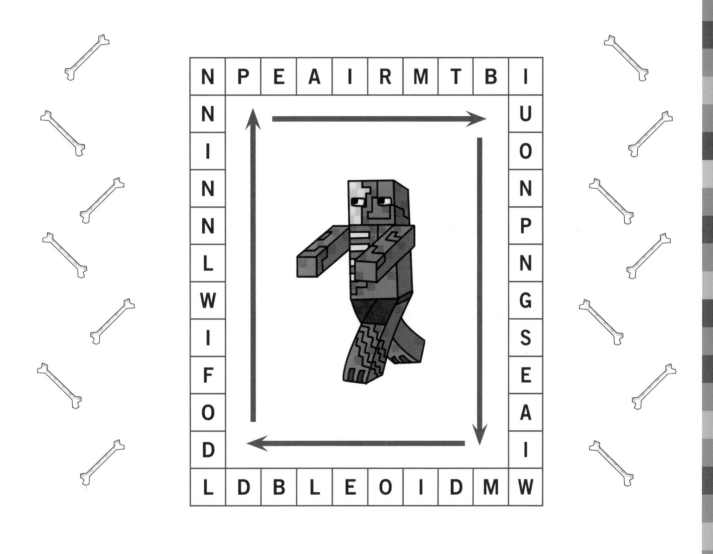

N	P	E	A	I	R	M	T	B	I
N									U
I									O
N									N
N									P
L									N
W									G
I									S
F									E
O									A
D									I
L	D	B	L	E	O	I	D	M	W

"_____ _____

_____ _____ _____"

ANSWER KEY

PAGE 152-153   ON THE PLAYGROUND

PAGE 154   ENCHANTED MAP

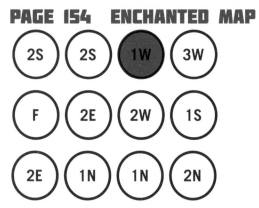

The red button is the first one pressed.

PAGE 155   COMMON CODE

NETHERRACK, GLOWSTONE, SOUL SAND
These things are found only in the Nether

PAGE 156
EVERY NOOK AND CRANNY

Start

Stop

PAGE 157
CIRCLE OF TRUTH: SURVIVAL TIP
WEAR A PUMPKIN ON YOUR HEAD AND ENDERMEN WON'T GET ANGRY WITH YOU

PAGE 158   SKELETON TWINS

PAGE 159
CONNECT THE DOTS: PIT OF PERIL

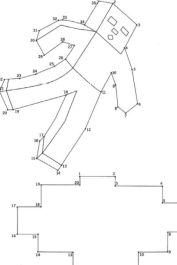

PAGE 160
SQUARED UP: BLOCK PARTY

S	I	G	C	O	D
O	C	D	S	G	I
I	O	S	D	C	G
D	G	C	O	I	S
C	S	I	G	D	O
G	D	O	I	S	C

PAGE 161
HOLD IT!

TORCHES CAN SUPPORT ANY AMOUNT OF WEIGHT

PAGE 162
COLLECTING TREASURE

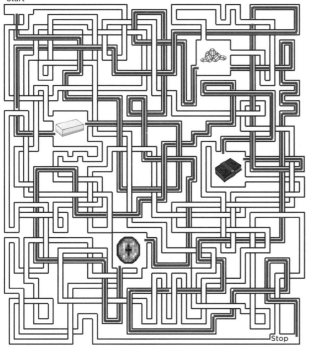

PAGE 163
CIRCLE OF TRUTH: FOOD FOR THOUGHT

EATING PUFFERFISH CAUSES POISONING, HUNGER, AND NAUSEA

PAGE 165
TIP FOR ENDING ENDERMEN

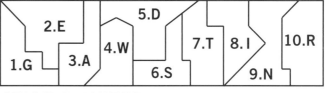

STAND IN WATER

PAGE 166
WORD FARM

PAGE 167
CONNECT THE DOTS: FARM LIFE

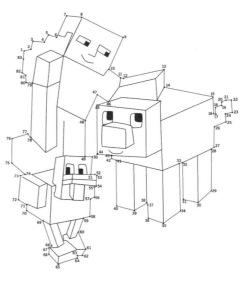

PAGE 168
HUNT FOR ENCHANTMENTS

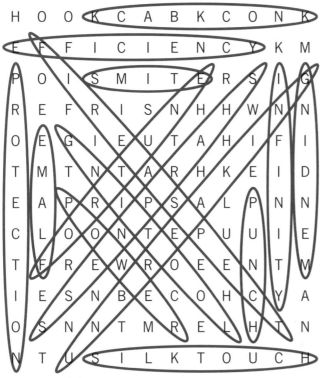

Unused letters:

HOOK MORE FISH WITH THE LURE ENCHANTMENT

PAGE 169
ROTTEN LUCK

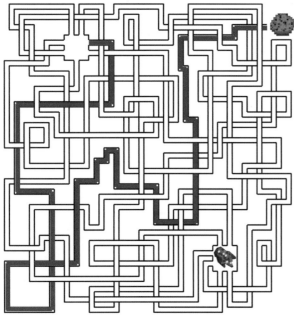

PAGE 170–171
MULTIPLAYER MISMATCH

PAGE 172
TWIN MOBS

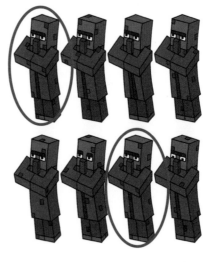

PAGE 173
PATH OF DOOM

*Gianna - Lava; Mason - Skeleton; Aya - Spider; **Demarco - Creeper**; Logan - Falling*

PAGE 174
TRUTH OR TALE?

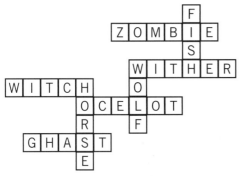

*THE HIGHER THE WOLF'S TAIL,
THE HEALTHIER IT IS*

This tall tale (about a tall tail!)
is true.

PAGE 175
CONNECT THE DOTS: OUR HERO

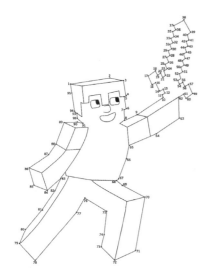

PAGE 176–177
TERMS OF THE GAME

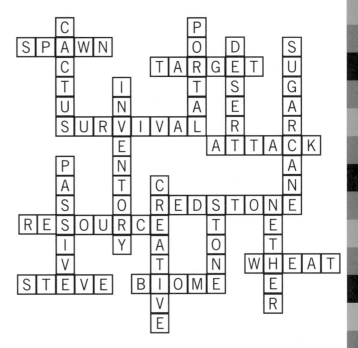

PAGE 178
SQUARED UP: INVENTORY

W	S	P	C	M	A
M	C	A	W	S	P
P	A	S	M	C	W
C	M	W	A	P	S
S	W	C	P	A	M
A	P	M	S	W	C

PAGE 179
FACT-FINDING MISSION
*NAMING A MOB "DINNERBONE"
WILL FLIP IT UPSIDE DOWN*
You start in the top left corner.

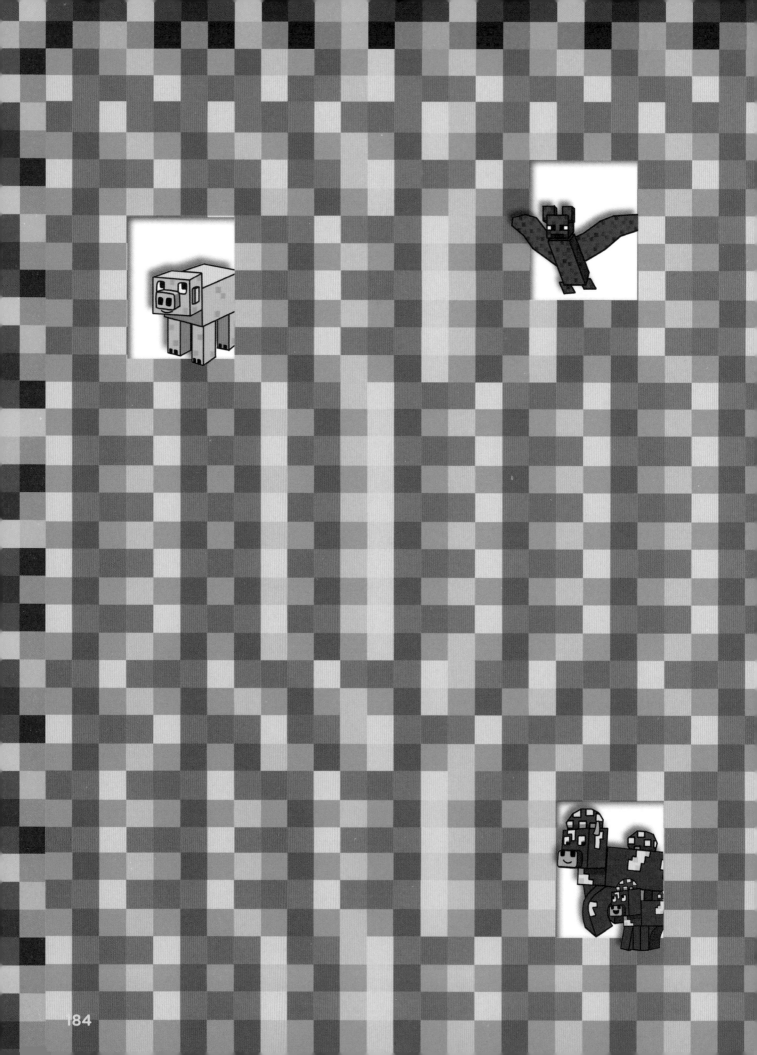

LANGUAGE ARTS FOR MINECRAFTERS

Cursive

a   *Apple*

a   *a   a   a   a*

a   apple

Blaze

b   *blaze*

b   *b*   *b*   *b*   *b*

C

Creeper

C c c c c

c creeper

1 2 *c*   *c*   *c*   *c*   *c*

Diamonds

d *diamonds*

d d d d d

$\mathcal{E}$ Ender dragon

$\mathcal{E}$ $\mathcal{E}$ $\mathcal{E}$ $\mathcal{E}$ $\mathcal{E}$

ender dragon

F

Fishing rod

F

f  *fishing rod*

f *f* *f* *f* *f*

Guardian

g guardian

g *g* *g* *g* *g*

H   Husk

h husk

2 3
1 *h* *h* *h* *h* *h*

I   *Iron golem*

218

i

iron golem

i   1 2 3

i   *i*   *i*   *i*

J

Jockey

j

jockey

j *j* *j* *j* *j*

K

Killer bunny

K K K K K

k *killer bunny*

L

Lapis lazuli

L

l   lapis lazuli

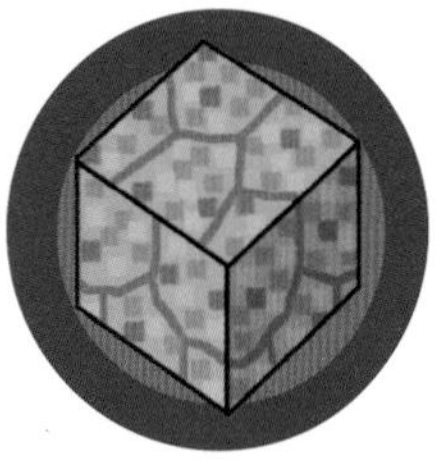

ℓ   *l*   *l*   *l*   *l*

M Mooshroom

m

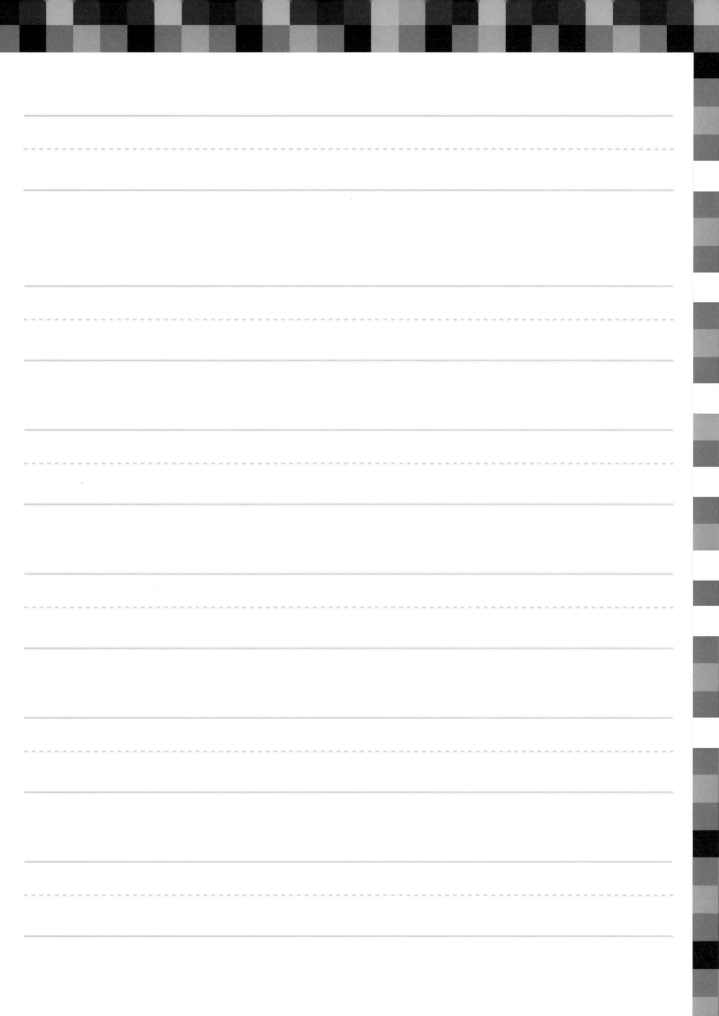

m  mooshroom

m

n

Nether wart

n *n* *n* *n* *n*

n   nether wart

$\mathcal{O}$ $\mathcal{O}celot$

ocelot

1 2 3

$\mathcal{P}$  $\mathcal{P}ortal$

$\mathcal{P}$ $\mathcal{P}$ $\mathcal{P}$ $\mathcal{P}$ $\mathcal{P}$

p

portal

$\mathcal{Q}$ Quartz

$\mathcal{Q}$ $\mathcal{Q}$ $\mathcal{Q}$ $\mathcal{Q}$ $\mathcal{Q}$

q

quartz

1 2 3 4 *q*

q *q* *q* *q*

R *Resources*

resources

$\mathscr{S}$  $\mathscr{S}lime$

s slime

s s s s s

T.N.T.

t   *t. n. t.*

3 → 2
1 → *t*   *t*   *t*   *t*   *t*

$\mathcal{U}$ $\mathcal{Upside\ down}$

$\mathcal{U}$ $\mathcal{U}$ $\mathcal{U}$ $\mathcal{U}$ $\mathcal{U}$

$\mathscr{U}$ upside down

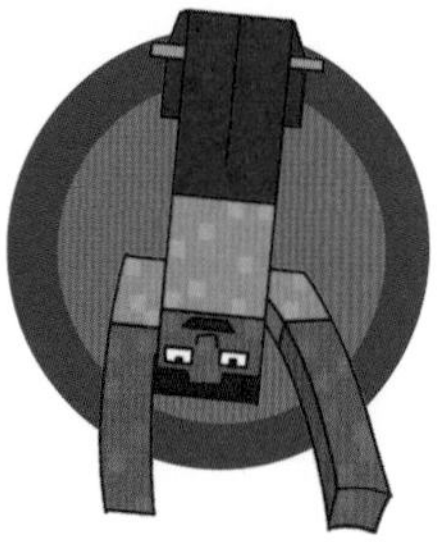

$\mathscr{u}$

$\mathcal{V}$

$\mathcal{V}illager$

1 2
$\mathcal{V}$

$\mathcal{V}$ $\mathcal{V}$ $\mathcal{V}$ $\mathcal{V}$ $\mathcal{V}$

$\mathcal{U}$ villager

$\mathcal{U}$ $\mathcal{U}$ $\mathcal{U}$ $\mathcal{U}$ $\mathcal{U}$

$\mathcal{W}$

Wolf

$\mathcal{W}$ $\mathcal{W}$ $\mathcal{W}$ $\mathcal{W}$ $\mathcal{W}$

$\mathcal{w}$

$wolf$

1 2 3 4 $\mathcal{w}$

X

X-ray mod

x  x-ray mod

Y   *Yellow*

1 2 3 *Y*   *Y*   *Y*   *Y*   *Y*

y *yellow*

1 2
y *y* *y* *y* *y*
3

$\mathcal{Z}$

Zombie

pigman

1→ 2↓ $\mathcal{Z}$ $\mathcal{z}$ $\mathcal{z}$ $\mathcal{z}$ $\mathcal{z}$

Z

zombie

pigman

1
2
Z   *Z*   *Z*   *Z*   *Z*

REVIEW THE ALPHABET

Practice the whole alphabet below!

NAME PRACTICE

Practice writing your name on the lines below and at right.

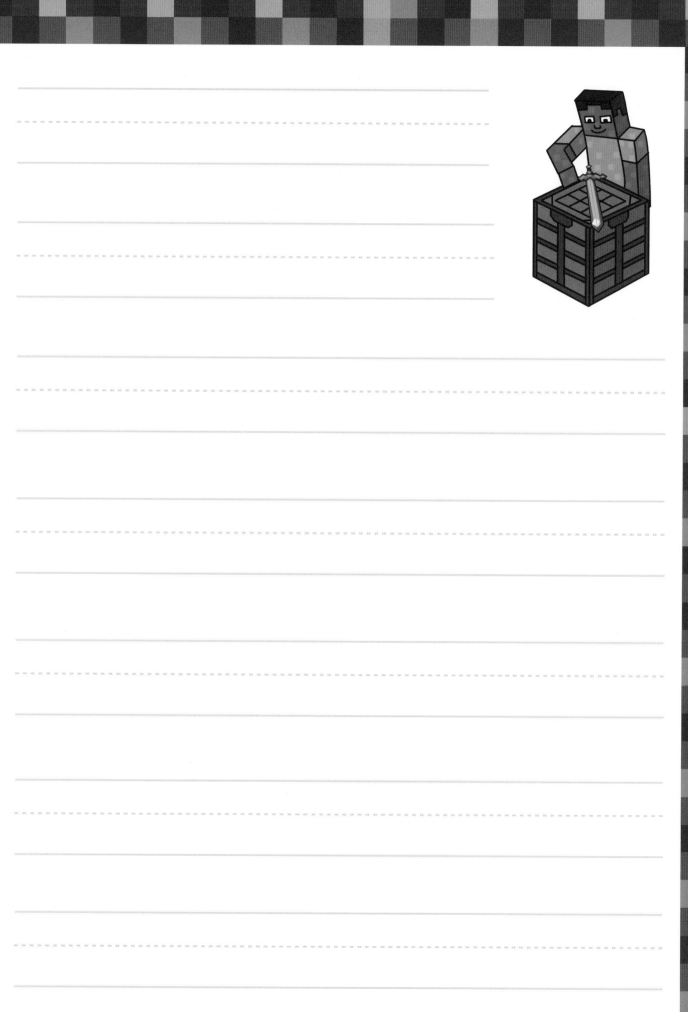

SENTENCE PRACTICE

Copy each sentence on the line below.

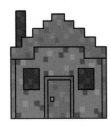 *Try to build a*

shelter by nightfall.

 *If you don't, a*

zombie will get you.

Chop trees to

get wood for a shelter.

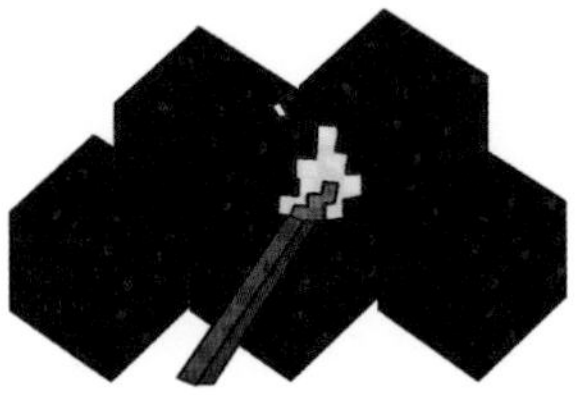

You'll need a

torch when it's dark.

Watch out for spiders!

Zombies burn

up in the daylight.

Skeletons shoot

their arrows at you.

Throw a splash potion!

Explore the

Nether if you dare.

Find the treasure

chest filled with emeralds

and diamonds.

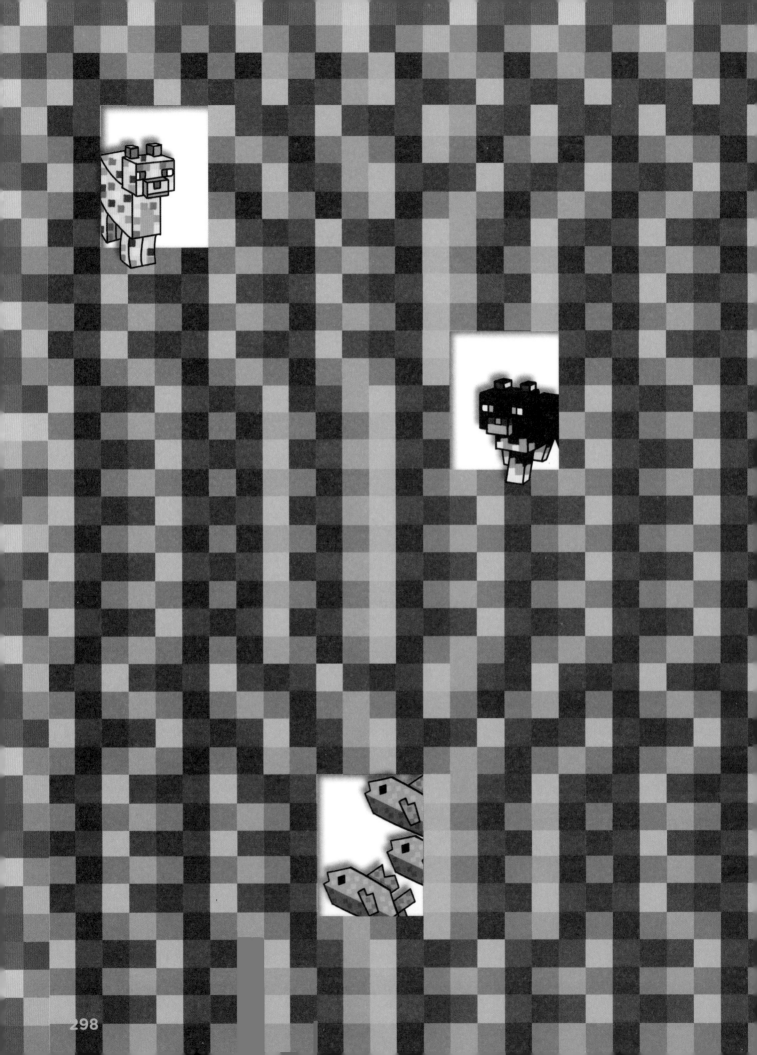

LANGUAGE ARTS FOR MINECRAFTERS

READING

PREFIXES

A prefix comes at the beginning of a complete word and turns it into a new word.

un   re   de   under   over   out

1. *Fill in the blank spaces with the new word.*

un + pack = _____   under + take = _____

de + fuse = _____   over + do = _____

re + read = _____   out + live = _____

2. *Choose the correct word to complete the sentences below.*

A. The program shut down and now I have to _____ it.
[remake / reopen]

B. I made a mistake building my tower, so I think I'll _____ it.
[undo / defrost]

C. After I'm done using a pressure plate, I can _____ it.
[deactivate / refinish]

D. The creeper headed toward me but I _____ it.
[underbid / outran]

SUFFIXES

A suffix comes at the end of a word. These suffixes help you make comparisons. When a root word ends in *y*, the *y* changes to an *i* when a suffix is added.

er   **est**   **ier**   **iest**

1. *Number the words in each column below in the order of least to most.*

_____ loud   _____ funnier

_____ loudest   _____ funny

_____ louder   _____ funniest

2. *Fill in the blank spaces below.*

smart + _____ = smarter

hard + <u>er</u> = _____

cool + _____ = coolest

happy + <u>er</u> = _____

sunny + _____ = sunniest

long + <u>est</u> = _____

PREFIXES

A prefix comes at the beginning of a complete word and turns it into a new word.

1. *Use the prefixes below to complete the sentences.*

mis   ir   dis   co

A. Susan _____ liked playing in Creative mode.

B. Jack _____ judged the location of his first shelter.

C. The kids would have to _____ operate to gather all the resources they needed.

D. It was _____ responsible of that griefer to steal their best items.

E. Their parents would _____ approve if they knew the kids had gone over their screen time limits.

F. Jack and Susan _____ agreed about whether they should trade the emeralds to a villager.

2. *Use each of the prefixes and one of the nouns to create four new words.*

Prefixes   mis   ir   dis   re

Nouns   **cover**   **regular**   **place**
         rational   **appear**   **trust**

_____   _____

_____   _____

SUFFIXES

A suffix comes at the end of a complete word and turns it into a new word.

1. *Use the suffixes below to complete the sentences.*

ful   less   ness   ment

A. Steve was brave and fear_____ as he battled the Ender Dragon.

B. When Alex opened the chest, she was blinded by the bright_____ of the diamonds.

C. Steve explored the base_____ of the villager's house.

D. Alex felt help_____ when she was outnumbered by a group of skeletons.

E. She stared at the giant zombie in amaze_____.

F. He used a potion of Weak_____ on the cave spider to reduce its strength.

2. *Use each of the suffixes and one of the nouns to create four new words.*

Suffixes	ful	less	ness	ment
Nouns	hope	base	light	care
	sad	dark	home	enjoy

_____   _____

_____   _____

VOWEL-CONSONANT-E SPELLING PATTERN

When a word or the final syllable of a word ends in *e*, then the first vowel is usually long and the *e* is silent.

Examples:

tap + e = tape   mop + e = mope

bit + e = bite   cub + e = cube

1.  *Circle the words that fit the vowel-consonant-e pattern.*

chase	smelt	make	brew
teleport	slime	cake	cast
blaze	plank	steep	tame

2. *Write four new words that fit the vowel-consonant-e pattern.*

_____   _____

_____   _____

SUFFIX –ING SPELLING PATTERN

If the root word has one short vowel sound and one final consonant (like 'pat'), then double the final consonant before adding 'ing'.

pat + ing = patting

let + ing = letting

sit + ing = sitting

chop + ing = chopping

run + ing = running

1. *Spell the following words using the -ing suffix.*

A. cut + ing = _____

B. dig + ing = _____

C. fan + ing = _____

D. bed + ing = _____

E. stop + ing = _____

F. plan + ing = _____

G. stun + ing = _____

H. trip + ing = _____

2. *Fill out the chart, writing the original word before the suffix -ing was added.*

	-ing	winning
	-ing	mapping
	-ing	getting
	-ing	wagging

305

PLURAL NOUN SPELLING PATTERNS

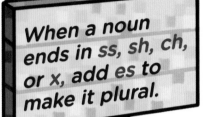

When a noun ends in *ss, sh, ch,* or *x,* add *es* to make it plural.

Examples:

grass + es = grasses

fish + es = fishes

rich = es = riches

1.

A. box= _____

B. kiss= _____

C. match = _____

D. bush = _____

E. mix = _____

F. witch = _____

G. crash = _____

H. lunch = _____

2.

	-es	sandwiches
	-es	wishes
	-es	catches
	-es	hoaxes

HOMOPHONES

> **Remember:** *Homophones* are words that sound the same but have different meanings.

1. *Use the words from the box to complete each sentence.*

their	they're	there

A. The kids are playing in _____ school's playground.

B. In a few minutes, _____ going to play a game of tag.

C. The school is over _____.

2. *Use the words from the box to complete each sentence.*

too	to	two

A. Cassie drew _____ clouds.

B. Enrico wants _____ go home soon.

C. "I want to play _____," said James.

3. *Select the correct word to complete each sentence.*

A. "What are you drawing over _____?" Dennis asked.
[here / hear]

B. "What? I didn't _____you," Cassie said. **[here / hear]**

C. "Is that _____ basketball?" Penny asked. **[your / you're]**

D. "_____ going to be late getting home," Enrico warned.
[your / you're]

SYNONYMS

Remember: Two words that have the same meaning are *synonyms*.

The Zombie Trap

Read the passage about zombies.

Zombies are so slow and lumbering that it is easy to escape them. Their low, groaning sounds alert you that they are nearby. Another way to <u>elude</u> a zombie is to stay in the sun. Zombies prefer the shade because sunlight will <u>obliterate</u> them in a matter of seconds. Zombies can <u>summon</u> other zombies to <u>expedite</u> an attack on their enemies. If a zombie attacks you, it can <u>transform</u> you into a zombie too.

1. *Write the <u>underlined</u> word from the passage that is the same as each definition below.*

   A. Turn into = _____　　**B.** Destroy = _____

   C. Get away from = _____　　**D.** Speed up = _____

   E. Call, gather = _____

2. *Find a word in the passage that is a synonym for the words below.*

   A. Warn, signal = _____　　**B.** Harm, strike = _____

   C. Foes, rivals = _____

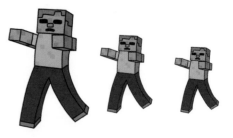

ANTONYMS

> **Remember:** Two words that have opposite meanings are *antonyms*.

3. *Write the <u>underlined</u> word from the passage that is the opposite of each definition below.*

A. Make better = _____

B. Keep the same = _____

C. Send away = _____

D. Catch, tackle = _____

E. Slow down = _____

4. *Find a word in the passage that is an antonym for the words below.*

A. Capture, find = _____

B. Distant, far away = _____

C. Quick, speedy = _____

SYNONYMS

Remember: Two words that have the same meaning are *synonyms*.

Creepers Really Creep Me Out

Read the passage about creepers.

A **horde** of creepers can be **exceptionally** quiet, so you need to be alert at all times. Creepers will sneak up on you and then **detonate** themselves. This will **demolish** anything near the blast. However, there is an easy way to protect yourself. Creepers are **petrified** of cats, so keep a cat with you at all times. Creepers also like to hide in caves, so beware any dark, hidden areas where one could be lurking.

1. *Match each **bold** word from the passage to its* synonym.

Horde   Explode

Exceptionally   Scared

Detonate   Mob

Demolish   Very

Petrified   Ruin

2. *Find a word in the passage that is a* synonym *for the words below.*

A. _____ Explosion, boom

B. _____ Defend, shield

C. _____ Concealed, unseen

ANTONYMS

> **Remember:** Two words that have opposite meanings are *antonyms*.

3. *Select the* antonym *from the list of words and write it on the line next to the **bold** word from the passage.*

implode	few	lots	slightly	fix
fearless	extremely	destroy	scared	explode

Horde _____

Exceptionally _____

Detonate _____

Demolish _____

Petrified _____

4. *Find a word in the passage that is an antonym for the words below.*

A. _____ Hard, difficult

B. _____ Loud, noisy

C. _____ Bright, sunny

VOCABULARY DEVELOPMENT

Read the passage about the Ender Dragon.

The Ender Dragon

The Ender Dragon <u>appears</u> in each world's End. Black with <u>glowing</u> violet eyes, she spits Ender acid from her mouth. The Ender Dragon circles in the air until she swoops down at a player, <u>charging</u> for the player's lower waist. In the process, she destroys any blocks she passes through, except for obsidian, bedrock, iron bars, and End stone. When a player kills an Ender Dragon, she drops experience orbs, <u>activates</u> the exit portal, and <u>spawns</u> a dragon egg on top of the portal. The exit portal leads to the Outer End.

1. *Match the underlined word from the story to a word in the box that has a* similar *meaning.*

shining	stops	arrives	reproduces
triggers	rushing	divides	

Appears _____   Spawns _____

Charging _____   Glowing _____

Activates _____

2. *Find a word in the passage that is* similar *to the words below.*

A. Doorway, entrance _____

B. Dives, plunges _____

C. Destroys, exterminates _____

VOCABULARY DEVELOPMENT

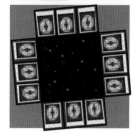

3. Connect the underlined word from the story to the word that has the opposite meaning.

Appears   Retreating

Charging   Vanishes

Activates   Dim

Spawns   Disables

Glowing   Destroys

4. Find a word in the passage that is different *from the words below.*

A. Upper, topmost   _____

B. Swallows, sips   _____

C. Picks up   _____

DEFINING WORDS BY CONTEXT

Remember: *Context* means the text surrounding a word. If you don't know a word, you can sometimes figure out what it means by the words around it.

Read the passage about gardening. Then choose a word from the passage that matches each definition.

Gardening

Steve will need plenty of food. The best way to get sustenance is to grow a garden of fresh vegetables. First he will need to assemble a wooden hoe to dig the garden. This hoe requires two sticks and two pieces of lumber as well as a crafting table. He will also need seeds for the types of vegetables he wants to plant. Finally, he will need a bucket to hold water and a torch to put next to his crops to provide light.

When Steve has his inventory together, it is time to till the soil. He clears a piece of land to make it level. Then he puts the hoe in the ground and drags it toward him, turning over a couple of inches of soil. He makes evenly spaced furrows to hold the seeds, allowing enough room for the plants to spread out. Steve distributes the seeds evenly in the rows, and then covers them lightly with soil.

Next, it's time to excavate a hole in the ground for water. Steve transfers water into the hole with his bucket. Then he puts the torch next to his crops to impart light. The torch will also deter monsters from consuming his plants.

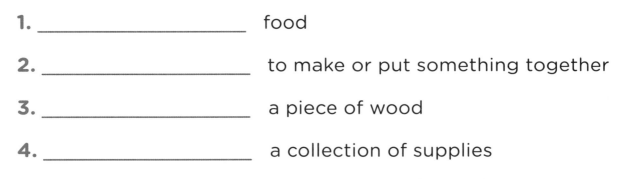

1. _____ food

2. _____ to make or put something together

3. _____ a piece of wood

4. _____ a collection of supplies

1. *Circle the letter that is the best description for the word from the passage.*

Require
   a. give   **b.** take   **c.** need

Provide
   a. take away   **b.** offer   **c.** shine

Till
   a. plow   **b.** plant   **c.** water

Distribute
   a. give out   **b.** hold   **c.** gather

Excavate
   a. create   **b.** dig   **c.** cover

Impart
   a. hide   **b.** give off   **c.** brighten

Deter
   a. prevent   **b.** invite   **c.** scare

2. *Read the sentences from the passage. Then circle the word in blue that means the same thing as the word in bold.*

A. He clears a piece of land to make it **level**. [flat / at an angle]

B. Steve **transfers** water into the hole with his bucket.
   [drizzles / moves]

C. The torch will also deter monsters from **consuming** his plants.
   [digging up / eating]

DEFINING WORDS BY CONTEXT

Read the passage about diamond armor. Then choose a word from the passage to complete the definitions.

Diamond Armor

Diamond armor is the strongest covering for a Minecrafter. This durable armor protects a player from many types of damage. It will shield you from fire, arrows, lava, cacti, lightning, and explosions. However, it will not shield you from suffocation if you are stuck inside a block or starvation if you run out of food.

You will need 24 diamond units to craft a full set of armor. You will need 5 diamonds to make a helmet and 8 diamonds to make a chestplate. To make leggings you will need 7 diamonds. Boots are made with 4 diamonds. Armor can be enchanted to provide even more protection.

Diamonds are most common in layers five through twelve. Look for their glint in lava lakes and water streams. You will need an iron pickaxe to mine for diamonds.

1. _____ very strong

2. _____ harm, injury

3. _____ having no food to eat

4. _____ having no air to breathe

DEFINING WORDS BY CONTEXT

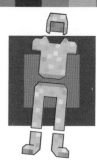

1. *Complete the chart using words from the passage.*

	make, create
	protect, defend
	given a charm
	shine, sparkle
	dig up
	protective covering
	blast, burst

2. *Write your own definitions for the words below.*

A. Chestplate: _____

_____

B. Common: _____

_____

MAIN IDEA AND DETAILS

Remember: The *main idea* is what the passage is about. The *details* support the main idea.

Read about igloos. Then answer the questions below.

Igloos

Igloos make a great pit stop if you are traveling. You will find them in cold, snowy biomes, such as the Ice Plains and Cold Taiga. If you get cold or hungry, you might be able to find an empty igloo to hang out in for a while. Inside will be a cozy room with everything you need. It will have a rug, a crafting table, a torch, and a heater. It will have lots of food stored on a shelf. You will also find blankets and warm clothes. Just watch out for polar bears!

1. What is the main idea of this text?

_____

_____

_____

2. List three details that support the main idea.

A. _____

B. _____

C. _____

MAIN IDEA AND DETAILS

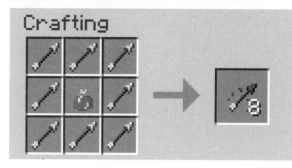

Read about tipped arrows. Then answer the questions below.

Tipped Arrows

Tipped arrows are arrows drenched with one of the potions. They'll give your victim the potion's effect, but only up to one-eighth of the time the original potion lasted. Here's the catch: the potion you use to create a tipped arrow has to be a lingering potion. A lingering potion is any splash potion that has been brewed with a bottle of dragon's breath. And to get the dragon's breath, well, you have to fight the Ender Dragon. And fighting the Ender Dragon is not easy!

1. The main idea of this text is:

   A. Tipped arrows are easy to make.
   B. Tipped arrows have no effect.
   C. Tipped arrows are hard to make.

2. One detail that supports the main idea is:

   A. You need a lingering potion to make a tipped arrow.
   B. Tipped arrows last only one-eighth of the time as the original potion.
   C. Tipped arrows are drenched in a potion.

3. Another detail that supports the main idea is:

   A. You need dragon's breath to make a lingering potion.
   B. Tipped arrows give your victim the potion's effect.
   C. Tipped arrows are the best way to defeat the enemy.

4. Another detail that supports the main idea is:

   A. A lingering potion is made from an original potion.
   B. You'll need to fight an Ender Dragon to get dragon's breath.
   C. Ender Dragons are easy to fight.

COMPARE AND CONTRAST

> **Remember:** When you *compare* two things, you are finding ways they are similar. When you *contrast* two things, you are finding ways they are different.

Read about skeletons and zombies. Then answer the questions.

Skeletons and Zombies

Skeletons like to travel in mobs. They will burn in sunlight, so they try to stay in the shade as much as possible. However, a skeleton will be protected from the sun if it is wearing a helmet. Skeletons drop bones and arrows. They are unable to see through glass. Skeletons are one of the harder mobs to defeat. A single skeleton can spawn almost anywhere in the Overworld at a light level of 7 or less.

Zombies are often found in mobs. Sunlight can kill a zombie but a helmet will protect it. Zombies drop rotten flesh, carrots, and potatoes. They move very slowly, so it is easy to defeat them. Zombies cannot see through glass. In the Overworld, zombies spawn in groups of four.

1. Compare

List three things that skeletons and zombies have in common.

1. _____

2. _____

3. _____

2. Contrast

List three ways that skeletons and zombies are different.

1. _____

2. _____

3. _____

POTIONS

Read about potions. Then fill out the chart.

Potions

Potions give you special powers. To make potions, you must collect certain items from the Nether. You also need to have a brewing stand. Almost all potions start with a base potion. When you add a particular ingredient to the base potion, you get a particular effect.

Glistering melon gives you instant health. Its icon is a slice of watermelon. Pufferfish lets you breathe underwater. Its icon is a pufferfish. A spider eye makes the potion poisonous. Its icon is a red spider eye. Sugar gives you speed. Its icon is a sugar crystal. A golden carrot gives you night vision. Its icon is a yellow carrot. A ghast tear, which has the icon of a teardrop, gives you regeneration. You get strength from blaze powder. This icon looks like a small fire.

Glistering melon	
	Pufferfish
Spider eye	
	Sugar crystal
Golden carrot	
Ghast tear	
	Fire

CAUSE AND EFFECT

Each ingredient in a potion causes an effect. Using the passage, match the cause with its effect by writing the correct letter on the line.

Cause

_____ Glistering melon

_____ Pufferfish

_____ Spider eye

_____ Sugar

_____ Golden carrot

_____ Ghast tear

_____ Blaze powder

Effect

A. Speed

B. Night vision

C. Strength

D. Poisonous

E. Instant health

F. Breathe underwater

G. Regeneration

ORDER OF EVENTS: GOING FISHING

Read the story about Will and Mina going fishing. Then on the next page number the events in the story in the order in which they happened.

Will stared at the bobber, hoping it would dip into the water. And then it did! He yanked back on the pole and started reeling in his catch.

It was big. It was heavy. It was round and yellow. It was . . . a pufferfish.

"No!" said Will. "Are you kidding me?"

As he unhooked the fish from his line, he heard Mina laughing from behind.

"Hey, you caught a big one!" she teased.

Will shot her a dirty look. "Maybe your bad luck with the cat is rubbing off on me. Did you catch him yet?"

Mina shook her head. "But he'll be back," she said with a smile. "Till then, I'll hang out with you."

Great, thought Will. He was about to toss the pufferfish back into the water when Mina held out her hand.

"Wait!" she said. "I can use that fish to make a potion—the potion of water breathing. My bottle is almost empty."

Will shrugged. "Be my guest," he said, tossing her the fish. Then he cast his line again into the water, hoping for better luck.

The bobber ducked underwater instantly. "Already?" said Will, gripping his pole. "Please don't be a pufferfish. Please don't be a pufferfish," he chanted as he reeled in the line.

As the fish broke the surface of the water, he breathed a sigh of relief. It was a beautiful pink salmon. He could almost taste it now! But as he unhooked the fish, Will had an uneasy feeling—like he was being watched.

From Lost in the Jungle: Secrets of an Overworld Survivor, Book 1 by Greyson Mann, Sky Pony Press, 2017.

ORDER OF EVENTS GOING FISHING

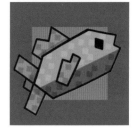

Number the events in the story in the order in which they happened.

_____ Will hopes he doesn't catch a pufferfish.

_____ Mina teases Will.

_____ Will gives Mina the fish.

_____ Will blames Mina for his bad luck.

_____ Mina holds out her hand for the fish.

_____ Will unhooks the salmon.

_____ Will casts his fishing line.

_____ Will reels in a salmon.

_____ Will feels uneasy.

_____ Will reels in a pufferfish.

ORDER OF EVENTS: WILL & THE PIG

Read the story about Will and the pig. Then on the next page number the events in the story in the order in which they happened.

This is it, thought Will. It's now or never. He leaned over the fence to scratch the pig's head, and then he reached for the saddle.

Oops! He'd almost forgotten the bait! "Wait here," he said to the pig. "I'll be right back."

Will grabbed his fishing pole and hurried to the garden to find a ripe carrot. As he tugged the leafy green end of one from the dirt, the pig grunted.

"Easy, boy," said Will, pressing his fishhook through the carrot. "You can eat it, but not quite yet." Then he hurried back to the pigpen and leaned the fishing pole against the fence. The carrot dangled just out of the pig's reach.

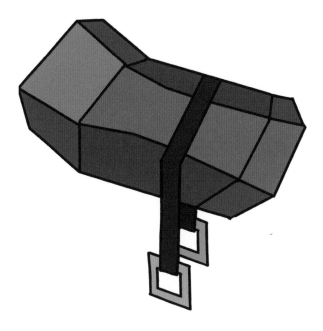

As Will placed his saddle gently on the pig's back, the pig grunted a protest. But he kept his black eyes on the carrot.

Will eased himself over the fence and lowered himself onto the saddle. Then he reached for the fishing pole.

"Okay, boy," he said. "Here we go. Follow the carrot!"

Will held the carrot just in front of the pig's nose, leading him left and right around the pen. The pig moved slowly at first and then began to trot. Will held on tight, laughing out loud. It was working. He was actually riding a pig!

From <u>Lost in the Jungle: Secrets of an Overworld Survivor</u>, Book 1 by Greyson Mann, Sky Pony Press, 2017.

ORDER OF EVENTS: WILL & THE PIG

Number the events in the story in the order in which they happened.

_____ Will puts the saddle on the pig.

_____ Will digs up a carrot.

_____ Will grabs his fishing pole.

_____ Will puts the carrot on the fishhook.

_____ Will gets into the saddle.

_____ The pig begins to trot.

_____ Will hurries back to the pigpen.

_____ Will holds the carrot in front of the pig's nose.

WHO, WHAT, WHEN, WHERE, WHY, HOW

Read the story about Lucy and Eric battling the skeletons. Then answer the questions.

"I need a sword!" Lucy cried out, looking frantically at the skeletons.

Eric crouched on the ground in the forest. The sun had set a long time ago, and it was hard to see. He felt through his inventory and found his spare sword. It wasn't ideal, but at least he could give something to Lucy. He hoped it would do. He handed it to Lucy.

"I'm sorry, but I only have a wooden sword."

"That's better than nothing! Thanks!"

Eric started to battle the skeletons with his powerful diamond sword, which he always fought with. He sprinted toward the two skeletons that Lucy had cornered. With a blow from his diamond sword, he defeated one of them. Lucy battled the other one with her wooden sword until it was destroyed.

"We make a great team," Eric said with a smile.

"The fight's not over yet," Lucy said as six new skeletons suddenly appeared and shot arrows at them. Eric's response was cut off as an arrow pierced his leg.

Lucy ran over to her friend and splashed a potion of Invisibility on him. Now the skeletons wouldn't be able to shoot more arrows at Eric.

"We need to find the spawner before it makes more skeletons. Let's go!"

Adapted from Skeleton Battle: The Unofficial Minecrafters Academy Series, Book 2, Sky Pony Press, 2016

1. Draw arrows pointing to the words in the passage that answer this question: **Who are the main characters in the story?**

2. Draw a triangle around the words in the passage that answer this question: **What are the main characters battling?**

3. Underline the words in the passage that give a clue to the answer to this question: **What time of day does this story take place?**

4. Draw a circle around the word in the passage that answers this question: **Where does the arrow pierce Eric?**

5. Draw a wavy line underneath the words in the passage that answer this question: **Why does Lucy say, "The fight's not over yet"?**

6. Draw a rectangle around the words in the passage that answer this question: **How are the skeletons multiplying?**

WHO, WHAT, WHEN, WHERE, WHY, HOW

Use full sentences to answer the following questions about the passage.

1. *Who* are the main characters in the story? _____

_____

_____

2. *What* are the main characters battling? _____

_____

_____

3. *What time of day* does this story take place? _____

_____

_____

4. *Where* does the arrow pierce Eric? _____

_____

_____

5. *Why* does Lucy say, "The fight's not over yet"? _____

_____

_____

6. *How* are the skeletons multiplying? _____

_____

_____

MAKING INFERENCES

> **Remember:** *Inference* is using facts, observations, and logic to come to an assumption or a conclusion. It is not stating what is obvious, or what has clearly been said. Using clues in the text, ask yourself: "What conclusions can I draw about an event or a character?"

Abby's Workshop

Abby loves to make things in her workshop. She has many tools hanging neatly on the wall, including a saw, hammer, and pliers. She keeps a box on the desk to hold small items, such as nails and screws. This makes it easy to find what she needs.

She has another box high up on a shelf. This box is for items that she doesn't need all the time. Plus, some of the things in the box can be harmful if swallowed, such as glue. She keeps them up high so her dog will not get into them. Her dog, Tootsie, is curious about everything and often gets into trouble. She will lick or eat just about anything!

The lamp on the desk is for when Abby works on small projects. The lamp helps her see details better, and it keeps her from squinting. She also needs good light so she can sweep up sawdust at the end of the day.

Abby's stool is always tucked under the desk when she isn't using it. She doesn't want her baby brother to trip over it. Sometimes she babysits him when her mom and dad are busy. She likes to take him into her workshop and show him what she is making. She hopes when he gets older he'll want to learn how to make things too. Then she will teach him how to use the tools and they will make things together. As long as he keeps her workshop just the way she likes it!

MAKING INFERENCES

For every inference you make, give three clues from the text.

1. What can you infer about Abby's character traits? _____

_____

_____

2. What are three clues in the text that helped you draw this inference?

_____

_____

3. What can you infer about the types of projects Abby makes?

_____

_____

4. What are three clues in the text that helped you draw this inference?

_____

_____

5. What can you infer about how Abby feels toward her brother?

_____

_____

6. What are three clues in the text that helped you draw this inference?

_____

_____

MAKING INFERENCES

Viktor's Room

Viktor's room is a mess and his dad won't let him go out until he cleans it. Viktor complains that it's his sister Sarah's fault.

"Sarah left her doll on the floor!" he yells.

"Besides that, whose games and books are on the floor?" his dad patiently replies.

"I don't know how those got there! The guys must have left it when they came over the other day."

Viktor's father isn't buying it. "What about your unmade bed?" he asks, trying to hide his smile. "Did the guys do that too?"

"Probably! They were wrestling, so they must have knocked the covers off!"

Viktor's father shakes his head and sighs. "You still have to clean it up before you go out."

Viktor stomps into his room. He mutters under his breath about his sister and his friends. Then he starts throwing books onto his bookshelf and slamming drawers. Suddenly the door opens and Sarah walks in.

"I'll help you, Viktor." She picks up her doll and starts to put the games away. Viktor watches her for a minute. He remembers how he blamed his room on her, and she's just a little kid.

"Thanks," he says. "I'll take you out for ice cream after we clean up, okay?"

MAKING INFERENCES

For every inference you make, give three clues from the text.

1. What can you infer about Viktor's character traits? _____

_____

_____

2. What are three clues in the text that helped you draw this inference?

_____

_____

3. What can you infer about how Viktor's father is feeling?

_____

_____

4. What are three clues in the text that helped you draw this inference?

_____

_____

5. What can you infer about how Viktor feels at the end of the story?

_____

_____

6. What are three clues in the text that helped you draw this inference?

_____

_____

UNDERSTANDING SETTING

> **Remember:** The *setting* is where a story takes place. A story can have one setting or many settings.

Read the passage. Then answer the questions.

It all started with brussels sprouts.

Tonight is my first night at Mob Middle School, which has me kind of creeped out. It's a time when a guy could really use a pork chop—burned to a crisp, just how I like it. But instead, Mom served me brussels sprouts!

See, she's all into this new cookbook: *30 Days to a Greener You*. Dad tells her, "Honey, you're as green as the day I met you." But that just makes her all weepy-eyed. Then they end up kissing or something. (GROSS!)

So let me say that I am not a fan of this green diet. Creepers don't eat brussels sprouts. It's not normal!

...I would have fed them to my pet dog, except I don't have one. I have a pet squid named Sticky.

And if I tried to feed them to Sticky, Mom would notice the gross green hunks floating in the aquarium. So I tried to feed them to my baby sister when Mom wasn't looking. But Cammy just threw them across the floor like bouncy balls.

When Dad scolded her, she scrunched up her face and did what she always does. She blew up. Yup, right there at the kitchen table. I almost wished I'd died in the blast and respawned somewhere else—like in a normal family's kitchen.

From The Creeper Diaries: Mob School Survivor by Greyson Mann, Sky Pony Press, 2017.

UNDERSTANDING SETTING

1. Write your answers to the questions below.

    A. What is the setting for the story?

    _____

    _____

    B. Give two clues that tell you where the setting is.

    _____

    _____

    C. Do you think this story might have another setting later on? If so, where might it be?

    _____

    _____

    D. What is the clue that tells you where a second setting might be?

    _____

    _____

2. Underline the words below that could be a setting for a story.

    a dentist's office   a friend   reading a book

    a bike store   a playground   playing

    the Overworld   your teacher   your bedroom

CHARACTERS

> **Remember:** *Characters* are the actors in a story. The narrator tells the story from his or her point of view. The *narrator* is often the main character.

Read the passage. Then answer the questions.

Well, the night started out okay. When Sam and his dad came to pick me up, my family wasn't TOO embarrassing. Except the Fashion Queen came downstairs wearing some stinky new gunpowder perfume.

I told Sam that my sister, Cate (a.k.a. the Fashion Queen) was trying to impress some guy named Steve. Sam laughed and said that her plan might not work, because Cate smelled like rotten eggs.

I don't really think Sam is one to talk, after that spoiled milk spilled all over him at school. But I let it slide. I've been doing that a lot with him lately.

Things were going pretty much okay until we got to Sam's house near the swamp. That's when three mini slimes bounced out of the house to greet us. Sam patted them all on their little slime heads.

TRIPLETS? As much as Sam talks, you'd think he might have mentioned that he has three little brothers.

Let's just say that I'm not a fan of little kids. They're loud and germy. Those mini Sams were oozing slime EVERYWHERE. I didn't want to touch anything!

But things got worse when we went inside the house. I smelled it before I saw it—a CAT. Here's what you should know about me and cats: we don't get along. Not at all.

Adapted from <u>The Creeper Diaries: Mob School Survivor</u> by Greyson Mann, Sky Pony Press, 2017.

CHARACTERS

Remember: Character *traits* are the parts of a person's personality. Readers get clues about a character's traits by how the person acts, thinks, and talks. A character trait is not an emotion or a feeling; feelings come and go, but traits are part of who a person is.

Reread the passage on the previous page. Then fill out the chart based on what you know about these three characters.

narrator		
Sam		
"Fashion Queen" Cate		

CONFLICT

Remember: In a story, the *conflict* is an event, a person (or people), or a situation that stands in the way of a character's achieving his or her goal. The conflict forces the character to take action in some way.

Read the passage below, and then answer the questions.

Warren rushed over to Lily. "What's going on?"

"The zombies keep spawning," Lily cried.

The sky was growing dark. Warren suggested, "You can stay at my house. We can't be out here now. It's too dangerous."

It was too late. An army of zombies marched through town, striking any villager who was in their path. The vacant-eyed mob ripped doors from their hinges, forcing the villagers to flee from their homes.

Lily checked her inventory. She had enough potions and arrows. Lily sprinted toward the zombie army with her diamond sword and slammed it against as many zombies as she could hit. Warren splashed potions on the zombies, weakening them. He aimed his bow and arrow and shot arrows into the mob. A villager fought alongside Warren and Lily, but she was hit by a fireball and destroyed. They were outnumbered.

"What are we going to do?" Lily cried. She was starting to panic. If she didn't destroy this mob of zombies, she would never make it back home again. She desperately wanted her family—her mom and dad, her cat, even her younger brother. If only she and Warren could find a way to defeat the mob and keep them from spawning.

Adapted from Mobs in the Mine: An Unofficial Minetrapped Adventure, Book 2, by Winter Morgan, Sky Pony Press, 2016.

CONFLICT

Reread the passage on the previous page. Then answer the questions that follow.

1. What is the main conflict in the story?

_____

_____

2. What is the conflict preventing the character from achieving?

_____

_____

3. What type of conflict does the story show?
Circle the correct answer.

    A. Conflict between the hero and nature
    B. Conflict between the hero and herself
    C. Conflict between the hero and others

4. Another type of conflict that could come out later in this story might be:

    A. Conflict between Lily and Warren
    B. Conflict between Lily and a terrible thunderstorm
    C. Conflict between Lily and her own fear
    D. All of the above

PLOT STRUCTURE

Remember A *plot* starts with an introduction, then has rising action, reaches a climax, has falling action, and finally comes to a resolution.

Read the passage below, and then answer the questions.

Mud flew this way and that as Will dug madly into the earth. He knew that thunderstorms were bad news. Not only would monsters spawn, but they could be super charged by lightning. He had to finish his shelter right now.

He heard the moans of two zombies before he saw them. Two—no, three—staggered across the ground, arms outstretched. Will pulled out his bow and launched arrows, one after another. The first zombie dropped with a grunt.

Will's heart pounded as he turned back toward his shelter. Zombies are slow, he told himself. I can make it—I can finish this in time. He dug out a few more blocks of dirt. Then he grabbed his bow and arrow and whirled around again.

Yikes! The two zombies were just a few feet away. Will dropped his bow and grabbed his sword instead. He stepped forward, swinging the sword. With a few strong strokes, he took down the first monster. The iron sword was amazing!

With a surge of confidence, Will attacked the second zombie. The monster growled and groaned before falling backward, dropping chunks of rotten flesh.

Will pumped his sword toward the sky. "Yeah!" he shouted. "Take that, you dirty mobs!"

Will turned and ran back. He was able to finish his shelter before any other mobs attacked.

Adapted from Lost in the Jungle: Secrets of an Overworld Survivor, Book 1 by Greyson Mann, Sky Pony Press, 2017.

PLOT STRUCTURE

Reread the passage on the previous page and then answer the questions.

1. Describe the introduction in the passage.

_____

_____

_____

2. What is the rising action in the passage?

_____

_____

_____

3. What is the passage's climax?

_____

_____

4. Describe the falling action in the passage.

_____

_____

_____

5. Explain the resolution in the passage.

_____

_____

_____

READING FLUENCY

Read the following passage out loud to practice your reading fluency. Use the chart on the next page to record how many words you can read correctly in a minute! Reread the passage every few days to track your progress.

Cave Spiders

To defeat the cave spider, you need to kill existing and spawning spiders and disable or destroy the spawner itself. Because they are so fast, you will be using a sword against them instead of the bow. This is because the bow takes several moments to pull and charge before you can fire an arrow.

You will find yourself trying to battle these spiders at the same time as trying to destroy enough cobwebs around the spawner so that you can disable it. You can use a bucket of water to remove cobwebs, and shears are the fastest tool to cut them. Water will also uproot any torches placed on the ground, so be aware of where your torches are.

One tactic is to close off the ends of the area where you know there's a spawner, and then tunnel in just above or below the spawner. Then you can quickly destroy it with your pickaxe or place torches on either side. Placing torches will create enough light that it prevents spiders from spawning.

Try to avoid letting these spiders get above you, where they can jump on you and damage you. The venom from their bite will cause you enough damage to bring you down to a half-heart of health. It won't kill you, but it will leave you very weak. Once you are bitten, retreat and use potions or milk to heal before you strike again. If you don't care about losing the spawner or any drops and experience points, you can pour a bucket of lava on it.

*Adapted from Hacks for Minecrafters: Combat Edition by Megan Miller, Sky Pony Press, 2014.

READING FLUENCY CHART

Have an adult help you chart your reading fluency.

1. Set a timer for one minute and start reading until the minute is up. Mark your stopping point on the passage. (Fast readers can count the words they read in 30 seconds and multiply that number by two.)

2. A friend or adult records the "words wrong" info on the chart below as you read.

3. Subtract the number of words you got wrong from the total number of words you read. This is called the "Words Correct Per Minute" (WCPM) number.

Words I Missed:

READING FLUENCY

Read the following passage to practice your reading fluency. Use the chart on the next page to record how many words you can read correctly in a minute! Reread the passage every few days to track your progress.

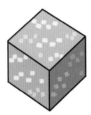

The Ice Biome

"Let's get going," said Jack. "We want to get to the cold biome before dark."

"Maybe we can build an igloo once we're there," suggested Toby.

The group trekked toward the cold biome and walked up a large mountain. Harriet paused at the top of the mountain. "I wonder if we could spot William's town from up here."

Jack searched the landscape, looking for signs of life. "I feel just like William and Oliver. It is beautiful up here."

Toby stared at the icy biome that was on the other side of the mountain. "I can't wait to slide on the ice. It looks like so much fun. And I want to have a snowball fight."

"We don't have time for silly games," scolded Harriet. "We're here to find William."

The gang made their way down the steep mountain toward the ice biome. They passed an unusually tall patch of snow and Harriet was the first to go over to check it out.

Toby took out a shovel and began to dig. "I'm looking for treasure," he joked, but he did think the patch of snow seemed out of place and was wondering if someone might have buried something beneath it. After unearthing a journal earlier that day, he was curious about what other things they could find in the Overworld.

Harriet joined Toby. "Let's place a hopper here for the snow to collect in." She set one up right next to them. Jack started digging too.

"I see something!" Angela shouted to the others.

"What is it?" asked Jack.

"I think it's a chest," said Toby.

"Open it!" Jack and Harriet stood next to him, waiting.

Toby opened the chest. "Blue helmets! It's filled with blue helmets!"

From <u>Discoveries in the Overworld: Lost Minecraft Journals</u>, Book 1 by Winter Morgan, Sky Pony Press, 2015.

READING FLUENCY CHART

Have an adult help you chart your reading fluency.

1. Set a timer for one minute and start reading until the minute is up. Mark your stopping point on the passage. (Fast readers can count the words they read in 30 seconds and multiply that number by two.)

2. A friend or adult records the "words wrong" info on the chart below as you read.

3. Subtract the number of words you got wrong from the total number of words you read. This is called the "Words Correct Per Minute" (WCPM) number.

Words I Missed:

READING FLUENCY

Read the following passage to practice your reading fluency. Use the chart on the next page to record how many words you can read correctly in a minute! Reread the passage every few days to track your progress.

The Attack of Mr. Anarchy

Lily grabbed the potion of Harming from her inventory and doused Mr. Anarchy.

"Attack him!" she called out to the others.

Michael and Simon stormed over to Mr. Anarchy, striking the sinister villain with their diamond swords.

"Stop!" Mr. Anarchy called out. "I'll tell you what you want to know."

They didn't listen to Mr. Anarchy. They struck him with their swords, just as two skeletons spawned in the small prison cell.

"Oh no!" Mr. Anarchy yelled. A skeleton shot an arrow at Mr. Anarchy.

"We have to get out of here!" Lily called to her friends.

The group darted from the prison. They scurried down the hall of the jungle temple, dodging arrows from the blue griefers that monitored the hall.

"Faster!" Lily cried to the group.

They ran as fast as they could until they exited the jungle temple. Lily hid behind a large patch of leaves. The others joined her. They grabbed their bows and arrows from their inventories and shot arrows at the blue griefers.

Then Michael spotted someone running past the soldiers.

"Do you see that person?" he asked the others.

"Yes," Simon responded, taking a second look at the person. "Mr. Anarchy must have respawned. We have to get out of here!"

Just then, skeletons and zombies spawned in the jungle temple, as magma cubes bounced toward the blue griefers. The gang hid behind the bark of a large tree and watched the blue griefers struggle to defeat the undead mobs and the cubes from the Nether.

*Text adapted from <u>Mobs in the Mine: An Unofficial Minetrapped Adventure</u> by Winter Morgan, Sky Pony Press, 2015

READING FLUENCY CHART

Have an adult help you chart your reading fluency.

1. Set a timer for one minute and start reading until the minute is up. Mark your stopping point on the passage. (Fast readers can count the words they read in 30 seconds and multiply that number by two.)

2. A friend or adult records the "words wrong" info on the chart below as you read.

3. Subtract the number of words you got wrong from the total number of words you read. This is called the "Words Correct Per Minute" (WCPM) number.

Words I Missed:

READING FLUENCY

Read the following passage to practice your reading fluency. Use the chart on the next page to record how many words you can read correctly in a minute! Reread the passage every few days to track your progress.

Minecrafting Enchantments

Enchanting and brewing potions can be challenging for beginners. Usually these activities will have to wait until you've gathered the proper resources. However, getting to this point should be a major goal if you want to survive well in Normal or Hard mode. Enchanted weapons and armor make a huge difference in surviving combat. They are absolutely necessary for fighting the strongest mobs, like the Ender Dragon and Wither.

Enchanting is easier than brewing potions because it doesn't require a trip to the Nether. To start enchanting, you need an enchantment table—which you craft from obsidian, books, and diamonds—and lapis lazuli to pay for the enchantments.

There are different levels for enchantments. For example, a Protection IV enchantment will give more protection than a Protection I enchantment. The level of enchantment you can give to an item is increased by surrounding the table with up to fifteen bookshelves.

To enchant, click on the enchantment table and place the item you want to enchant in the left slot. In the right panel, you'll be given three choices of enchantment. It will tell you how many experience levels you need to perform the enchantment, as well as how many lapis lazuli (and how many experience levels) it will cost.

Select the enchantment you want on the right and then remove your enchanted item. Sometimes you will get extra enchantments with the one you picked. Enchanted items have a magical glow.

Text adapted from Hacks for Minecrafters: Combat Edition by Megan Miller, Sky Pony Press, 2014

READING FLUENCY CHART

Have an adult help you chart your reading fluency.

1. Set a timer for one minute and start reading until the minute is up. Mark your stopping point on the passage. (Fast readers can count the words they read in 30 seconds and multiply that number by two.)

2. A friend or adult records the "words wrong" info on the chart below as you read.

3. Subtract the number of words you got wrong from the total number of words you read. This is called the "Words Correct Per Minute" (WCPM) number.

Words I Missed:

ANSWER KEY

PAGE 300

1. unpack
   defuse
   reread
   undertake
   overdo
   outlive
2. reopen
   undo
   deactivate
   outran

PAGE 301

1 loud	2 funnier
3 loudest	1 funny
2 louder	3 funniest

PAGE 302

A. dis
B. mis
C. co
D. ir
E. dis
F. dis

2. Answers may vary. Some answers include:

discover
irrational
reappear
mistrust
displace

PAGE 303

A. less
B. ness
C. ment
D. less
E. ment
F. ness

2. Answers may vary. Some answers include:

hopeful
basement
enjoyment
careless
darkness
sadness

PAGE 304

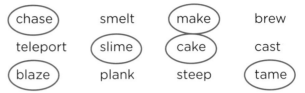

(chase)   smelt   (make)   brew
teleport   (slime)   (cake)   cast
(blaze)   plank   steep   (tame)

2. Answers may vary.

PAGE 305

1. A. cutting
   B. digging
   C. fanning
   D. bedding
   E. stopping
   F. planning
   G. stunning
   H. tripping

2.

win	-ing	winning
map	-ing	mapping
get	-ing	getting
wag	a-ing	wagging

PAGE 306

1. A. boxes
   B. kisses
   C. matches
   D. bushes
   E. mixes
   F. witches
   G. crashes
   H. lunches

2. Fill out the chart, writing the original word before the plural -es was added.

sandwich	-es	sandwiches
wish	-es	wishes
catch	-es	catches
hoax	-es	hoaxes

PAGE 307

1. The kids are playing in **their** school's playground. In a few minutes, **they're** going to play a game of tag. The school is over **there**.

2. Cassie drew **two** clouds.
   Enrico wants **to** go home soon.
   "I want to play **too**," said James.

3. **A.** "What are you drawing over **here**?" Dennis asked. [here / hear]
   B. "What? I didn't **hear** you," Cassie said. [here / hear]
   C. "Is that **your** basketball?" Penny asked. [your / you're]
   D. "**You're** going to be late getting home," Enrico warned. [your / you're]

PAGE 308

1. **A.** Turn into   **transform**
   B. Destroy   **obliterate**
   C. Get away from   **elude**
   D. Speed up   **expedite**
   E. Call, gather   **summon**

2. **A.** Warn, signal   **alert**
   B. Harm, strike   **attack**
   C. Foes, rivals   **enemies**

PAGE 309

3. **A.** Make better   **obliterate**
   B. Keep the same   **transform**
   C. Send away   **summon**
   D. Catch, tackle   **elude**
   E. Slow down   **expedite**

4. A. Capture, find   **escape**
   B. Distant, far away   **nearby**
   C. Quick, speedy   **slow**

PAGE 310

1.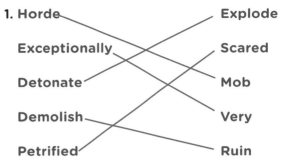
   Horde — Mob
   Exceptionally — Very
   Detonate — Explode
   Demolish — Ruin
   Petrified — Scared

2. **A.** **blast**   Explosion, boom
   B. **protect** Defend, shield
   C. **hidden**   Concealed, unseen

PAGE 311

3. Horde   **few**
   Exceptionally   **slightly**
   Detonate   **implode**
   Demolish   **fix**
   Petrified   **fearless**

4. **A.** **easy**   Hard, difficult
   B. **quiet** Loud, noisy
   C. **dark**   Bright, sunny

PAGE 312

1. Appears   **arrives**
   Charging   **rushing**
   Activates **triggers**
   Spawns   **reproduces**
   Glowing   **shining**

2. **A.** Doorway, entrance   **portal**
   B. Dives, plunges   **swoops**
   C. Destroys, exterminates   **kills**

PAGE 313

3.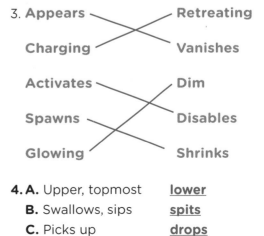
   Appears — Vanishes
   Charging — Retreating
   Activates — Disables
   Spawns — Dim
   Glowing — Shrinks

4. **A.** Upper, topmost   **lower**
   B. Swallows, sips   **spits**
   C. Picks up   **drops**

PAGE 314

1. **sustenance** food
2. **assemble** to make or put something together
3. **lumber** a piece of wood
4. **inventory** a collection of supplies

PAGE 315

1. Require   c
   Provide   b
   Till   a
   Distribute   a
   Excavate   b
   Impart   b
   Deter   a

2. A. **flat**
   B. **moves**
   C. **eating**

PAGE 316

1. **durable** very strong
2. **damage** harm, injury
3. **starvation** having no food to eat
4. **suffocation** having no air to breathe

PAGE 317

1.	craft	make, create
	shield	protect, defend
	enchanted	given a charm
	glint	shine, sparkle
	mine	dig up
	armor	protective covering
	explosion	blast, burst

2. A. Chestplate: **A piece of armor that protects the chest.**
   B. Common: **Ordinary, found everywhere**

PAGE 318

Note: Answers may vary. This is a sample of possible answers.

1. What is the main idea of this text?
The main idea of the text is that an igloo makes a good pit stop if you are in a snowy biome and get cold or hungry.

2. List three details that support the main idea.
A. Igloos have everything you need.
B. Igloos have food stored on shelves.
C. Igloos have blankets and warm clothes.

PAGE 319

1. C
2. A
3. A
4. B

PAGE 320–321

Note: Answers may vary. This is a sample of possible answers.

Compare

Skeletons and zombies travel in mobs.

Skeletons and zombies burn in sunlight.

Skeletons and zombies cannot see through glass.

Contrast

Skeletons drop bones and arrows; zombies drop rotten flesh, carrots, and potatoes.

Skeletons are hard to defeat; zombies are easy to defeat.

Skeletons spawn alone; zombies spawn in groups of four.

PAGE 322

Glistering melon	Watermelon
Pufferfish	Pufferfish
Spider eye	**Red spider eye**
Sugar	Sugar crystal
Golden carrot	**Yellow carrot**
Ghast tear	**Teardrop**
Blaze powder	Fire

PAGE 323

E   Glistering melon

F   Pufferfish

D   Spider eye

A   Sugar

B   Golden carrot

G   Ghast tear

C   Blaze powder

PAGES 324–325

7   Will hopes he doesn't catch a pufferfish.

2   Mina teases Will.

5   Will gives Mina the fish.

3   Will blames Mina for his bad luck.

4   Mina holds out her hand for the fish.

9   Will unhooks the salmon.

6   Will casts his fishing line.

8   Will reels in a salmon.

10 Will feels uneasy.

1   Will reels in a pufferfish.

PAGES 326–327

5   Will puts the saddle on the pig.

2   Will digs up a carrot.

1   Will grabs his fishing pole.

3   Will puts the carrot on the fishhook.

6   Will gets into the saddle.

8   The pig begins to trot.

4   Will hurries back to the pigpen.

7   Will holds the carrot in front of the pig's nose.

PAGE 328

"I need a sword!" Lucy cried out, looking frantically at the skeletons.

Eric crouched on the ground in the forest. The sun had set a long time ago, and it was hard to see. He felt through his inventory and found his spare sword. It wasn't ideal, but at least he could give something to Lucy. He hoped it would do. He handed it to Lucy.

"I'm sorry, but I only have a wooden sword."

"That's better than nothing! Thanks!"

Eric started to battle the skeletons with his powerful diamond sword, which he always fought with. He sprinted toward the two skeletons that Lucy had cornered. With a blow from his diamond sword, he defeated one of them. Lucy battled the other one with her wooden sword until it was destroyed.

"We make a great team," Eric said with a smile.

"The fight's not over yet," Lucy said as six new skeletons suddenly appeared and shot arrows at them. Eric's response was cut off as an arrow pierced his leg.

Lucy ran over to her friend and splashed a potion of Invisibility on him. Now the skeletons wouldn't be able to shoot more arrows at Eric.

"We need to find the spawner before it makes more skeletons. Let's go!"

PAGE 329

1. **Who are the main characters in the story?**
Lucy and Eric are the main characters in the story.

2. **What are the main characters battling?**
The characters are battling skeletons.

3. **What time of day does this story take place?**
The story takes place at night.

4. **Where does the arrow pierce Eric?**
The arrow pierces Eric in the leg.

5. **Why does Lucy say, "The fight's not over yet"?**
Lucy says, "The fight's not over yet" because six more skeletons appeared.

6. **How are the skeletons multiplying?**
The skeletons are multiplying from a spawner.

PAGES 330–331

Note: Answers may vary. This is a sample of possible answers.

What can you infer about Abby's character traits?

Abby is a neat and careful person. She is creative and kind.

What are three clues in the text that helped you draw this inference?

She shows she is careful by putting everything away neatly.

She shows she is creative by having a workshop and making projects.

She shows she is kind by looking out for her dog and her brother's safety.

What can you infer about the types of projects Abby makes?

Abby makes things out of wood.

What are three clues in the text that helped you draw this inference?

She has tools such as a saw, hammer, and pliers.

She keeps nails and screws in a box on her desk.

She sweeps up sawdust at the end of the day.

What can you infer about how Abby feels toward her brother?

Abby cares about her brother and wants to teach him how to make things when he is older.

What are three clues in the text that helped you draw this inference?

She tucks in her stool so her baby brother won't trip over it.

She likes to take her brother into her workshop and show him things.

She hopes he'll want to make things with her when he is older.

PAGES 332–333

Note: Answers may vary. This is a sample of possible answers.

What can you infer about Viktor's character traits?

Viktor is messy, blames other people for his mistakes, and gets angry easily.

What are three clues in the text that helped you draw this inference?

Viktor's room is a mess.

Viktor blames his friends and his sister for the way his room is.

Viktor stomps into his room and throws things around.

What can you infer about how Viktor's father is feeling?

Viktor's father is trying to be patient and reason with his son.

What are three clues in the text that helped you draw this inference?

He talks patiently to Viktor.

He points out that his friends probably didn't make the whole mess.

He shakes his head and sighs but says Viktor still has to clean his room.

PAGES 332–333 (CONTINUED)

What can you infer about how Viktor feels at the end of the story?

Viktor feels guilty when his sister comes to help him clean.

What are three clues in the text that helped you draw this inference?

Viktor realizes he blamed her for his mess.

Viktor knows she is just a little kid and doesn't deserve his blame.

Viktor says he will take her out for ice cream.

PAGES 334–335

1. **What is the setting for the story?**

The setting is the dinner table in the home of the narrator.

Give two clues that tell you where the setting is.

A. The mom is serving him brussels sprouts.

B. The baby sister blew up "right there at the kitchen table."

Do you think this story might have another setting later on? If so, where might it be?

Yes, I think the story will have a second setting at Mob Middle School.

What is the clue that tells you where a second setting might be?

The narrator says, "Tonight is my first night at Mob Middle School."

2. <u>a dentist's office</u>, a bike store, <u>the Overworld</u>, a friend, <u>a playground</u>, your teacher, reading a book, playing, <u>your bedroom</u>

PAGES 336–337

Note: Answers may vary. This is a sample of possible answers.

narrator	Grouchy	Doesn't like little kids, doesn't like cats, doesn't expect the night to go well
Sam	Good-natured Talkative	Jokes about rotten egg smell. Narrator says he talks a lot.
"Fashion Queen" Cate	Dramatic Cares about appearances	Likes attention, trying to impress Steve nickname is "Fashion Queen"

PAGES 338–339

1. What is the main conflict in the story?
   The main conflict is a battle between Lily and Warren and a mob of zombies.

2. What is the conflict preventing the character from achieving?
   The conflict is preventing Lily from going home.

3. What type of conflict does the story show?
   C. *Conflict between the hero and others*

4. Another type of conflict that could come out later in this story might be:
   D. *All of the above*

PAGE 340–341

1. Describe the introduction in the passage.
   The story starts with Will digging a shelter.

2. What is the rising action in the passage?
   The rising action starts when we learn that Will has to dig the shelter quickly because of the approaching thunderstorm and the zombies. Then the rising action continues with the zombies attacking and Will fighting them off.

3. What is the passage's climax?
   The climax is when Will destroys the last zombie.

4. Describe the falling action in the passage.
   The falling action starts when the last zombie groans and drops chunks of rotting flesh. The falling action continues with Will celebrating his victory.

5. Explain the resolution in the passage.
   The resolution is when Will is able to complete his shelter.

FOR MORE BRAIN-BUILDING FUN TRY THIS BOOK NEXT!

AN UNOFFICIAL QUIZ BOOK

THE KNOW-IT-ALL TRIVIA BOOK FOR MINECRAFTERS

BRIAN BOONE

ILLUSTRATED BY AMANDA BRACK